HERTFORDSHIRE
GARDEN HISTORY

A miscellany

HERTFORDSHIRE GARDEN HISTORY

A miscellany

Edited by Anne Rowe

HERTFORDSHIRE PUBLICATIONS
an imprint of the
University of Hertfordshire Press

First published in Great Britain in 2007 by
Hertfordshire Publications
an imprint of the
University of Hertfordshire Press
Learning and Information Services
University of Hertfordshire
College Lane
Hatfield
Hertfordshire AL10 9AB

Hertfordshire Publications, an imprint of the University of Hertfordshire Press,
is published on behalf of the Hertfordshire Association for Local History

The right of Anne Rowe to be identified as editor of this work has been asserted by her in accordance with
the Copyright, Designs and Patents Act 1988

British Library Cataloguing in Publication Data
A catalogue record for this book is available from the British Library

ISBN 978-1-905313-38-9

Design by John Robertshaw, AL5 2JB
Printed by Hobbs the Printers Ltd, Totton, Hampshire

Contents

List of figures

List of colour plates

Abbreviations

AGT	Association of Gardens Trusts
BL	British Library
BLO	Bodleian Library, Oxford
GHS	Garden History Society
HHA	Hatfield House Archive
HALS	Hertfordshire Archives and Local Studies
HGT	Hertfordshire Gardens Trust
RCHM	Royal Commission on Historical Monuments
RHS	Royal Horticultural Society
RIBA	Royal Institute of British Architects

Acknowledgements

The editor should like to thank the following people at Hertfordshire County Council for their help in the production of this book: Simon Odell, Head of Landscape, and Liz Heath in the Environment Department for their support and for providing a grant to help cover the cost of procuring some of the illustrations for the book; Sue Flood, County Archivist, for her support and editorial advice and for permitting us to reproduce images of maps and illustrations in her care; Steve Bayley, Mapping and GIS Officer, for providing digital images from the Council's aerial photomaps; and the staff at Hertfordshire Archives and Local Studies for their cheerful helpfulness at all times.

Published with the support of:

Hertfordshire County Council

Hertfordshire Gardens Trust

Preface

Since 1991, when the Hertfordshire Gardens Trust was founded, volunteer members have been researching the history of the county's parks and gardens. The earliest research project, directed by Dr Richard Bisgrove, resulted in the Trust's first publication – *Hertfordshire gardens on Ermine Street* (1996) – a mini-gazetteer of historic parks and gardens along the A10 in the east of the county. The present volume provides an opportunity to bring to wider attention one of the most important discoveries from that early research – the lost garden at Roxford near Hertingfordbury. Our next project examined the parks and gardens of west Hertfordshire, under the direction of Dr Tom Williamson. This research culminated in the Trust's most ambitious publication to date, *The parks and gardens of west Hertfordshire* (2000). As part of this project Alan Fletcher's keen legal brain spotted some anomalies in the hitherto accepted view that the early eighteenth-century landscape of Tring Park was designed by Charles Bridgeman. His reasoning and conclusions are published here for the first time.

Much of the work presented in this volume, however, was not undertaken at the instigation of the Hertfordshire Gardens Trust. Several members of the Trust's Research Group have, alongside their work for the Trust, attended a variety of academic courses in Garden History, leading to a range of qualifications in this popular subject. Most of the essays in this book have arisen from research, much of it original, undertaken as part of their coursework over the past few years.

Hertfordshire Publications were keen to publish a book about the county's garden history and it was Kate Harwood who came up with the excellent idea of a collection of essays. The result is here for you to enjoy. The book starts with an overview by Tom Williamson of what makes the history of Hertfordshire's parks and gardens different from anywhere else. Thereafter, the essays are arranged roughly chronologically, starting with an examination of a garden created in the seventeenth century and finishing with one created in the twentieth. In between are essays exploring a wide variety of different aspects of garden history in the county. All of them make a significant contribution to our ever-growing body of knowledge about the history of Hertfordshire and demonstrate the depth and breadth of some of the research which has been undertaken in recent years.

Anne Rowe
October 2006

CHAPTER ONE

The character of Hertfordshire's parks and gardens

Tom Williamson

Designed landscapes in Hertfordshire

At first sight Hertfordshire may not seem the most obvious hunting ground for those interested in historic parks and gardens. Large areas of the county are urbanised, or suburbanised; some of the most important country houses (Theobalds, Cashiobury, Panshanger) have been demolished; and a very high proportion of the remainder have been converted to institutional or commercial use and their grounds simplified or given over to housing developments, playing fields, or (in particular) golf courses. Yet, as this body of essays makes very clear, much of importance still survives, if on occasions in fragmentary form, including a number of landscapes by designers of particular note. Early geometric gardens generally remain (as in most parts of the country) only as fragments or archaeological traces, as at Hadham Hall or Standon Lordship; but the exceptions include such gems as St Paul's Walden Bury, with its elaborate woodland garden dating from the early eighteenth century, and Benington Park, with its spectacular terraced garden dating perhaps from the seventeenth century or earlier.[1] The simplified but still geometric designs of Charles Bridgeman are particularly well represented in the county, as we shall see; while, from the second half of the eighteenth century, Lancelot 'Capability' Brown's work at Ashridge survives in surprising condition and important elements of his work remain at Youngsbury, Moor Park, Kimpton Hoo and Pishiobury. Brown's neglected 'imitator' Nathaniel Richmond worked at Lamer, a site surviving still in good condition, as well as at six other Hertfordshire estates, including Hitchin Priory.[2] Richard Woods, another contemporary of Brown, carried out important work at Newsells and Brocket, as Esther Gatland describes in Chapter 7. Humphry Repton

Figure 1.1 Hertfordshire parks and gardens mentioned in this chapter. Those marked with a curly symbol are the subjects of subsequent chapters. © ANNE ROWE

undertook commissions at perhaps fifteen places in the county, including Panshanger and Wall Hall;[3] while high Victorian gardening is represented, above all, by the stunningly restored Ashridge. Later styles of garden, especially those in the 'arts and crafts' mode, are particularly well represented. Hertfordshire, in short, is surprisingly rich in historic parks and gardens. Moreover, the county has made its own distinctive contribution to the development of landscape design in Britain, both through notable individuals like Moses Cook, author of one of the most important treatises on forestry of the seventeenth century and gardener at Hadham Hall and subsequently Cashiobury, and through the products of particular firms, such as Pulham and Sons of Broxbourne and Sander's of St Albans. Pulham and Sons was one of the main manufacturers of artificial rockwork in the nineteenth century – discussed in some detail in this volume by Kate Banister (Chapter 8); and Frederick Sander, dealt with by Harold Smith in Chapter 9, was once the leading supplier of orchids in England.

So far I have concentrated on how national styles, and the works of designers with national reputations, are represented in the county: and this is the usual approach of garden historians to their subject. But we can also look at the history of designed landscapes in a rather different way. Rather than concentrate on how national developments were manifested in a particular area, we can take regional developments on their own terms and examine how particular districts have their own distinctive histories of landscape design.[4] Such histories were in part a consequence of the 'genius of the place' – of the special features of natural topography and earlier landscape history which ensured that each region or area presented its own opportunities and challenges to designers. But they were also the outcome of particular local social and economic histories, which determined the quantities of money and land available for garden-making in successive periods, ensuring, for example, that some phases of design might be better represented than others. Proximity or otherwise to the main centres of political and cultural influence might also affect the kinds of landscape found in a particular area at a particular time. To some extent such histories were also the consequence of patterns of social contact and emulation: the curious proximity of the eighteenth-century grottoes at Roxford and Amwell described by Patience Bagenal and Lottie Clarke (Chapters 5 and 6) may well be an example of this.

The genius of the place: landscape and topography

It is a commonplace among landscape historians and archaeologists that administrative counties make very poor units for the study of landscapes. Particular kinds of countryside seldom stop, in a convenient and obliging fashion, at county boundaries: they respond to the dictates of soils and topography in a way that administrative units seldom do. Hertfordshire is a striking example of this, for it is a peculiarly artificial entity.[5] The west of the county corresponds with the eastern end of the Chiltern Hills: a chalk escarpment with a long attenuated dipslope, covered by clay-with-flints and cut by widely spaced valleys. In early times this was sparsely settled ground, and extensive tracts of wooded common survived here into the early modern period. It was and is an area of scattered settlement, which once had extensive areas of open-field arable, although these were enclosed at an early date. This landscape extends, without interruption, westwards into Buckinghamshire and Oxfordshire: it has few if any features which are peculiar to Hertfordshire. The east of the county, in contrast, is boulder-clay country. Here the more diminutive north-eastern continuation of the Chiltern escarpment (the 'East Anglian Heights') has a long but much dissected dipslope covered with boulder clay, giving rise to fertile but heavy soils. This was a densely settled landscape even in medieval times, although numerous woods survived where the soils were heaviest. Settlement was again fairly scattered, often around diminutive greens, and as before this kind of countryside extends without interruption across the county boundary – into Essex, and beyond, into southern East Anglia. The south of the county is different again. Here the dominant formation is the London clays, giving rise to poor, leached and heavy soils, and again the distinctive features of the landscape (similarly characterised by much woodland and scattered settlement) extended without interruption into what was once Middlesex. Now London has eaten up Middlesex and it is the suburbs which extend without interruption across the county boundary, with only pockets of the old rural landscape still surviving.

There is thus no distinctive 'Hertfordshire landscape'. Yet the diverse landscapes of the county do display a number of shared features and these have had an important influence on the character of their designed landscapes. First, Hertfordshire has for the most part a rolling topography. Some relatively level areas do occur, especially on the wide interfluves between the principal valleys cutting through the dipslope of the Chilterns, but on the whole the terrain is relatively hilly, providing extensive prospects over vales and valleys which designers in all periods were keen to exploit. On the other hand, the county singularly lacks the kinds of rugged, soaring terrain which would have appealed to many eighteenth-century enthusiasts for the 'Picturesque'. Secondly, all the varied landscapes of Hertfordshire – those of its northern fringes excepted – are versions of 'woodland' or 'ancient countryside'.[6] All had a relatively dispersed pattern of settlement – there were always large numbers of isolated farms and small hamlets, as well as (or in some cases, instead of) nucleated villages. And all were enclosed into small fields from a relatively early date – sometimes because fields had been reclaimed directly from the woodlands and wastes in medieval times, industrialists, wishing to reside in convenient proximity to their enterprises, built houses and laid out gardens and parks nearby. John Dickinson, who owned several paper mills in the Gade valley, designed his own somewhat idiosyncratic house, Abbots Hill, in the parish of Abbots Langley.[20] Completed in 1837, it was accompanied by formal parterres and a small park typical of the period but, interestingly, the house stood on a hill above the valley and no attempt was made to hide Dickinson's mills, the canal or the railway line from view with judicious planting: Dickinson was clearly happy to include in the prospect these signs of modernity. His partner, Charles Longman, built the house of Shendish on the opposite side of the river: the park and gardens, laid out by Edward Kemp, similarly overlooked Apsley Mill below.[21] The incipient, spatially restricted industrialisation – mainly limited in the nineteenth century to the major valleys in the centre and south of the county – had other effects on the development of designed landscapes which would certainly repay further research. But designed landscapes and country seats also had a reciprocal relationship with the working landscape. The presence of two great houses, The Grove and Cashiobury – the homes of Lord Clarendon and the Earls of Essex respectively – ensured that the valley of the Gade between King's Langley and Croxley remained free from industry, and the London–Birmingham railway, constructed in 1837, was diverted away from its most convenient route, along the valley, through cuttings and a tunnel running through the higher ground to the east.[22]

The extent of early industrialisation should not be exaggerated. In the nineteenth century Hertfordshire remained an agricultural county, albeit one in which increasing numbers of the metropolitan rich made their homes. Indeed, it is arguable that until the later nineteenth century the presence of London actually served to suppress the growth of Hertfordshire's towns, which could not compete with the capital in the supply of many goods and services. This helps explain another noteworthy feature of the county's garden history: the absence of large mid-Victorian public parks of the kind which are relatively common, for example, in the great cities and conurbations of the industrial north. Public parks only began to appear in Hertfordshire at the end of the century and, as Harold Smith explains in his discussion of Clarence Park in St Albans (Chapter 10), by this time public spaces had become less elaborate and more functional in character than in previous decades –

more recreation ground than ornamental designed landscape.

As London expanded northwards in the later nineteenth century the kinds of residential patterns already outlined intensified. More and more successful businessmen chose to move out of the city, to establish homes in quieter, more rural places within easy reach of London by train. The pace of urban and industrial growth accelerated after 1900 and a contrast developed between the landscapes of south-west Hertfordshire, and those of the north-east. By 1941 Watford and Barnet were said to be 'largely dormitory areas for London in which the dwellers owe little allegiance to the old centres on the fringe of which they now reside'; while other places in the south and west of the county were described as having 'entered a new phase: fast and efficient transport to London and to the Midlands combined with a local labour supply have attracted many light industries and much of south west Hertfordshire has thus become greatly industrialised'. Such developments were 'less marked in the eastern two-thirds of Hertfordshire',[23] which remained largely rural. Urban expansion not only affected the kinds of designed landscapes which were created in the county in the later nineteenth and twentieth centuries, as we shall see. It also determined, in part, the extent to which, and ways in which, country houses and the parks and gardens associated with them have survived to the present. For those landowners whose seats were increasingly engulfed in suburban development the temptation to sell was considerable; 200 acres of the Oxhey Park estate were sold as building lots as early as 1866–72.[24] However, rising local population densities and the proximity of the capital often ensured that alternative uses could be found for grand houses and their grounds, and at a surprisingly early date. In 1880, only fifteen years after it had been built, the great Victorian mansion of Bushey Hall was turned into a therapeutic establishment.

By the early twentieth century local authorities in the south of the county were becoming aware of the need to preserve areas of open land for public recreation amidst the growth of suburbia. The break-up of the Cashiobury estate started in 1908, when 184 acres of the Home Park were sold to developers for detached middle-class housing. However, 75 acres were offered to Watford Council as a public park. More land was sold for development in the 1920s and the mansion was demolished in 1927, but the local authority was able to acquire more of the park and it remains a much-valued open area on the west side of Watford (Figure

1.4). The Brookmans Park estate (which had swallowed up the mansion – demolished *c*.1840 – park and gardens of Gobions) to the south of Hatfield was sold to developers in 1923. Hatfield Rural District Council decided in 1938 to buy part of what had been the Gobions estate as public open space but the Second World War intervened. The idea was subsequently revived and in 1956 North Mymms Parish Council acquired the site of the former Gobions mansion, together with its ornamental lake. In an attempt to preserve another part of the estate – an attractive area of woodland – from future development, local residents formed the Gobions Woodland Trust and, without fully appreciating the fact at the time, fortuitously purchased the land on which Charles Bridgeman had laid out his famous gardens in the early eighteenth century.[25] In 1937 Rickmansworth Urban District Council stepped in to prevent further speculative building development occurring on the seventeenth-century Moor Park by purchasing the mansion and 350 acres of the park, half of which was made into a golf course for members of the public.[26]

Figure 1.4 Cashiobury Park, Watford: transformed from private to public pleasure ground in the twentieth century, complete with typical park furniture. PHOTOGRAPH BY ANNE ROWE, 2006

By the second half of the twentieth century relatively few of the larger mansions in the county, and especially in the south and west of the county, remained in private, family ownership. Many had become schools, hotels and the like, and their grounds survived only in degraded condition. In particular, probably around thirty historic parks in the county are now occupied by golf courses: this could reasonably be described as another defining feature of the county's landscape heritage. On the other hand, while a number of large mansions were demolished outright during the course of the twentieth century – including Cashiobury and Panshanger – the developments described above ensured that there were probably fewer demolitions than in many more remote and rural districts, where stately piles could less easily be found new uses.

The proximity of London and the chronology of style
Proximity to London, and the regular influx of men and money from the capital, had important implications for the style as well as for the size and number of Hertfordshire's designed landscapes. In the seventeenth and eighteenth centuries national culture was strongly focused on London, on the court and on parliament. Taste was defined here: major designers and nurseries were based here. Indeed, until the early eighteenth century there were relatively few provincial nurseries. In the reign of Queen Anne the Brompton Park nursery, run by George London and Henry Wise, more or less monopolised the supply of plants to and the design of parterres for aristocratic gardens in England. As Stephen Switzer put it, 'Twill be hard for any of posterity to lay their hands on a tree in any of these kingdoms that have not been part of their care'.[27] George London advised on the layout of the grounds at Cashiobury, where the head gardener from 1669 was the great Moses Cook, who also worked for a while at the Brompton Park nursery (from 1681 to 1689: he was London's predecessor as Wise's partner).

Given the nearness of London, and the constant exodus of London money out into the county, it is not surprising that Hertfordshire landowners seem, for the most part, to have kept well abreast of the latest fashions. This is particularly true in the first half of the eighteenth century, as exemplified by such gardens as Hamels in east Hertfordshire, created by Ralph Freman MP in the 1710s: a bird's eye view, published in 1722, shows that the new wilderness here was already very 'informal' in style, with very sinuous paths (Figure 1.5).[28] George London's successor as Wise's partner, and Wise's successor as Royal Gardener from 1728, was Charles Bridgeman, a man who – like Wise before him – combined his official duties in and around the capital with an extensive private practice. He was one of the main pioneers in the 1720s and 30s of a simpler, less cluttered, stripped-down version of the formal garden, dominated by grass slopes and terraces, lawns, wildernesses and geometric bodies of water. Such gardens were now often more open to the surrounding landscape because they were surrounded, not by a continuous wall, but by a *fosse* or 'ha-ha'.[29] Bridgeman designed landscapes all over the country, but a significant proportion of his work, and especially of his smaller commissions, was in the vicinity of London. A designer might travel hundreds of miles to make a vast landscape for an Earl or Duke, but less far, perhaps, for a landowner of more modest means. Hertfordshire, not surprisingly, has a number of Bridgeman designs, the most important of which were Brocket, Moor Park, Sacombe, Briggens, Gobions and Tring. As Kate Harwood demonstrates in Chapter 4, at least four of these were created for men who had grown wealthy through direct or indirect involvement in the East India

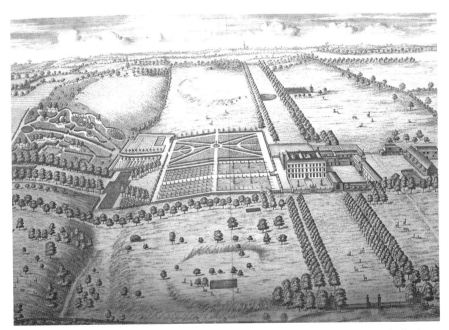

Figure 1.5 Hamels near Braughing by Thomas Badeslade, 1722. The serpentine paths in the wilderness on the left of the picture were at the cutting edge of garden design

Company. Tring Park is a particularly important landscape, whose complex history is examined with meticulous care by the late Alan Fletcher in Chapter 3.

The shift towards simpler, less formal forms of geometry partly pioneered by Bridgeman probably took hold in Hertfordshire, and in the other Home Counties, rather faster than in more distant and provincial areas of the country: and there were many other country seats, such as Beechwood in the Chilterns, where the new style was adopted wholesale in the 1730s and 40s. Insufficient research has yet been carried out to be certain, but on present evidence Hertfordshire gardens in the 1740s and 50s were perhaps a decade or more ahead of those in places like Norfolk or Lincolnshire.

By the 1750s and 60s, as is well known, a yet more 'informal' form of garden design was being widely adopted – the 'naturalistic' landscape style of Lancelot Brown and his 'imitators'. In this style, all straight lines and geometric features were eschewed and the park, rather than the garden, became the principal setting for the house. Several such landscapes are shown, albeit schematically, on Dury and Andrews' map of Hertfordshire (published in 1766 but surveyed over a number of previous years), for example at Bayfordbury, Stagenhoe near Whitwell, and Moor Place in Much Hadham, as well as at Brocket and Newsells, described by Esther Gatland in Chapter 7.[30] That map also, however, shows clearly that many landowners still retained more formal, geometric elements in their grounds, of the kind designed by Bridgeman or, indeed, by London and Wise (Figure 1.6). What is particularly striking is that these were not necessarily penniless backwoods squires, but major landowners, some of whom, like Earl Cowper at Cole Green Park, had already employed Brown to modernise their parks and gardens. Such retention of old-fashioned elements was, perhaps, most striking at Moor Park, where in spite of Brown's activities a complex mesh of avenues (many of them probably pre-dating Bridgeman's involvement at the site) survived, and is shown by Dury and Andrews. But the story was much the same at Ashridge, where the two avenues framing the south front of the house likewise survived Brown, as did the formal rides cut through the woods to the north. The same pattern is evident elsewhere: Cashiobury, Tring, Hamels, Tewin Water and Balls Park in Hertford all retained much of their geometric structure well into the second half of the eighteenth century. Evidently, many established

Figure 1.8 Some of the exotic animals kept in Tring Park in the early twentieth century.
REPRODUCED BY KIND PERMISSION OF HALS [POSTCARD IN PICTURE COLLECTION]

Conclusion

This short volume does not pretend to offer a comprehensive history of Hertfordshire's historic parks and gardens: that history will, of necessity, be a long time coming, for there is much that we still do not know or understand. But the essays presented here do show, very clearly, some of the rich and complex character of our heritage of designed landscape. They also serve to indicate the breadth and variety of the important research work currently being carried out by the members of the Hertfordshire Gardens Trust.

Notes

1. A. Rowe (ed.), *Garden making and the Freman family: a memoir of Hamels 1713–1733* (Hertford, 2001), pp. 57–60.
2. B. Howlett, *Hitchin Priory Park: the history of a landscape park and gardens* (Hitchin, 2004); D. Brown, 'Nathaniel Richmond (1724–1784) "Gentleman Improver", (PhD thesis, University of East Anglia, 2000).
3. S. Daniels, *Humphry Repton: landscape gardening and the geography of Georgian England* (Yale, 1999), pp. 260–1.
4. T. Williamson, 'Designed landscapes: the regional dimension', *Landscapes,* 5 (2004), pp. 16–24.
5. T. Williamson, *The origins of Hertfordshire* (Manchester, 2000), pp. 1–19.
6. O. Rackham, *The history of the countryside* (London, 1976), pp. 1–8.
7. A. Rowe, 'The distribution of parks in Hertfordshire: landscape, lordship and woodland', in R. Liddiard (ed.), *The medieval park: new perspectives* (Macclesfield, forthcoming).
8. A. Rowe, *Parks in Hertfordshire: the first 500 years* (Hatfield, forthcoming).
9. O. Rackham, 'Pre-existing trees and woods in country-house parks', *Landscapes,* 5 (2004), pp. 1–15.
10. The original map is lost but a copy survives among the archives at the house, now a school.
11. As shown, for example, on an estate map of 1785: HALS, DE/X736/E2.
12. D. Wratten, *The Book of Radlett and Aldenham* (Buckingham, 1990), p. 31.
13. HALS, DE/B1622/P3, plan of Kendals Hall, *c.*1740.
14. Hertfordshire Gardens Trust and T. Williamson, *The parks and gardens of west Hertfordshire* (HGT, 2000), pp. 44–5.
15. London School of Economics Coll Misc 38/3 fo.8.
16. Rackham, 'Pre-existing trees and woods'.
17. J. Bateman, *The great landowners of Great Britain and Ireland* (London, 1876), pp. 61, 154.
18. A. Young, *General view of the agriculture of Hertfordshire* (London, 1804), p. 18.
19. HALS, DZ/42/Z1, Red Book for Tewin Water.
20. J. Evans, *The endless webb: John Dickinson and Co.* (London, 1955), p. 55.
21. *Ibid.*, pp. 27–90; E. Kemp, *How to lay out a small garden* (London, 1858), pp. 241–5.
22. L.M. Munby, *The Hertfordshire landscape* (London, 1977), p. 217.
23. L.G. Cameron, *The land of Britain: Hertfordshire* (Land Utilisation Survey, London, 1941), p. 336.
24. J.E. Cussans, *History of Hertfordshire* 3 (Hertford, 1879–81), p. 175.
25. P. Kingsford, 'A history of Gobions in the parish of North Mymms', and L. Jonas 'The present: Gobions Woodland Trust', in P. Kingsford, R. Bisgrove and L. Jonas, *Gobions Estate North Mymms, Hertfordshire* (Brookmans Park, 1993), pp. 14, 17–21.
26. M. Pedrick, *Moor Park: the Grosvenor legacy* (Rickmansworth, 1989), p. 62.
27. S. Switzer, *Ichnographia rustica* 1, (London, 1718), p. 83.
28. Rowe (ed.), *Memoir of Hamels,* pp. xxiii, lxv.
29. P. Willis, *Charles Bridgeman and the English landscape garden* (London, 1977), p. 19.
30. HALS, A. Dury and J. Andrews, *A topographical map of Hartford-Shire* (1766; republished by the Hertfordshire Record Society in 2004).
31. Hertfordshire Gardens Trust and Williamson, *West Hertfordshire,* pp. 90–5.
32. Anon., *Gardener's Chronicle* (1885), pp. 37–8; Anon., *Gardener's Chronicle* (1893), pp. 131, 151; Anon., *Country Life* (1897), pp. 604–6.
33. HALS, Acc3898/26, Herts Gardens Trust file, extracts transcribed from the private diaries of Henry Hucks Gibbs, 'Aldenham House Yearbook 1871–1902'; A. Lawrence, *The Aldenham House gardens: a brief history of the school grounds* (Elstree, 1988), p. 29 (quoting *The Garden,* 10 May 1924).

Bibliography

Primary sources

Hertfordshire Archives and Local Studies (hereafter HALS), Acc3898/26, Herts Gardens Trust file, extracts transcribed from the private diaries of Henry Hucks Gibbs, 'Aldenham House Yearbook 1871–1902', in the possession of Lord Aldenham

HALS, AH/2770, 'A map of his Grace The Duke of Bridgewater's estate in the counties of Buckingham and Hartford' by G. Grey of Lancaster, 1762

HALS, DE/B1622/P3, plan of Kendals Hall, c.1740

HALS, DE/X629/P1, Bayfordbury Estate map, 1807

HALS, DE/X736/E2, Cashiobury estate map, 1798

HALS, Dury, A. and Andrews, J., *A topographical map of Hartford-Shire* (1766; republished by the Hertfordshire Record Society in 2004)

HALS, DZ/42/Z1, Red Book for Tewin Water, 1799

HALS, Picture Collection, postcard of Tring Park, early twentieth century

London School of Economics, Coll Misc 38/3, fo.8

Secondary sources

Anon., *Country Life* (1897)

Anon., *Gardener's Chronicle* (1885)

Anon., *Gardener's Chronicle* (1893)

Bateman, J., *The great landowners of Great Britain and Ireland* (London, 1876)

Brown, D., 'Nathaniel Richmond (1724–1784) "Gentleman Improver"', (PhD thesis, University of East Anglia, 2000)

Cameron, L.G., *The land of Britain: Hertfordshire* (Land Utilisation Survey, London, 1941)

Cussans, J.E., *History of Hertfordshire* 3 (Hertford, 1879–81)

Daniels, S., *Humphry Repton: landscape gardening and the geography of Georgian England* (Yale, 1999)

Evans, J., *The endless webb: John Dickinson and Co.* (London, 1955)

Hertfordshire Gardens Trust and Williamson, T., *The parks and gardens of west Hertfordshire* (HGT, 2000)

Howlett, B., *Hitchin Priory Park: the history of a landscape park and gardens* (Hitchin, 2004)

Jonas, L., 'The present: Gobions Woodland Trust', in P. Kingsford, R. Bisgrove and L. Jonas, *Gobions Estate North Mymms, Hertfordshire* (Brookmans Park, 1993)

Kemp, E., *How to lay out a small garden* (London, 1858)

Kingsford, P., 'A history of Gobions in the parish of North Mymms', in P. Kingsford, R. Bisgrove and L. Jonas, *Gobions Estate North Mymms, Hertfordshire* (Brookmans Park, 1993)

Lawrence, A., *The Aldenham House gardens: a brief history of the school grounds* (Elstree, 1988)

Munby, L.M., *The Hertfordshire landscape* (London, 1977)

Pedrick, M., *Moor Park: the Grosvenor legacy* (Rickmansworth, 1989)

Rackham, O., *The history of the countryside* (London, 1976)

Rackham, O., 'Pre-existing trees and woods in country-house parks', *Landscapes*, 5 (2004)

Rowe, A. (ed.), *Garden making and the Freman family: a memoir of Hamels 1713–1733* (Hertford, 2001)

Rowe, A., *Parks in Hertfordshire: the first 500 years* (Hatfield, forthcoming)

Rowe, A., 'The distribution of parks in Hertfordshire: landscape, lordship and woodland', in R. Liddiard (ed.), *The medieval park: new perspectives* (Macclesfield, forthcoming)

Switzer, S., *Ichnographia rustica* 1, (London, 1718)

Williamson, T., *The origins of Hertfordshire* (Manchester, 2000)

Williamson, T., 'Designed landscapes: the regional dimension', *Landscapes,* 5 (2004)

Willis, P., *Charles Bridgeman and the English landscape garden* (London, 1977)

Wratten, D., *The Book of Radlett and Aldenham* (Buckingham, 1990)

Young, A., *General view of the agriculture of Hertfordshire* (London, 1804)

CHAPTER TWO

The gardens at Quickswood, the hunting lodge of the Earls of Salisbury

Caroline Dalton

Introduction

Twenty-first century Quickswood sits in an elevated position on the hills to the east of Baldock in north Hertfordshire (Figure 2.1). Little more than a farm and some cottages, it is still surprisingly isolated, on a single-track road not far off the A507 from Buntingford to Baldock.

Quickswood was originally part of Clothall Manor and there is no separate record of it until 1572, when Thomas Perient of Digswell *'habuit manerium Quixsolt'*.[1] The manor descended through Thomas' daughter to the Burgoyne family. In the early seventeenth century it was owned by Nicholas Trott, a distant relative of the Burgoynes. Trott 'built the House of Quickswood which is a most agreeable Situation between the Champion and the Woodlands'[2] around 1600, but then sold it to William Cecil, second Earl of Salisbury, in 1617.[3]

The Cecils used Quickswood predominantly as a hunting lodge in the seventeenth and eighteenth centuries and contemporary accounts[4] demonstrate that there was a garden during this period. After the house was destroyed in 1780 the site became a farm, which it remains to this day.

Figure 2.1 Ordnance Survey map showing the location of Quickswood. EDINA DIGIMAP www.digimap.edina.ac.uk, 2005 ACCESSED 10/12/2005. © CROWN COPYRIGHT/DATABASE RIGHT 2005. AN ORDNANCE SURVEY/(DATACENTRE) SUPPLIED SERVICE

early in the century and he continued to supply plants to Quickswood over a number of years. The orchard was supplemented by more cherries and peaches in 1631, along with nectarines,[18] and in 1655 a further forty-three fruit trees were purchased, including pears and apricots, and John Easden was paid 27s for 'bringing dung out of the greens yard … for the chery trees when they are set'.[19] There are references to building an arbour in the 'Great Orchard' in 1661,[20] so it is possible that planting of fruit trees had expanded beyond the kitchen garden at this time.[21]

From the earliest evidence of Thomas Heath's plan it seems that an ornamental courtyard garden existed on the north-west front of Quickswood house, in addition to the productive kitchen garden and orchard. Andrews reported in 1909 that 'the walls of the garden can be traced, the one in the hedge on the left being still *in situ,* to a height of 2 feet'.[22] There is no indication of how this garden was laid out but it may have been in a style typical of an early seventeenth-century formal walled garden, perhaps with herb and flowerbeds surrounded by low box hedging, with gravel paths between them. There is reference in the accounts to the 'new gate for the walk before the house' in 1655;[23] this walk could have been a raised terrace giving views of the ornamental garden below. The major part of the garden beyond the courtyard, despite being on elevated ground with views to the north, was enclosed with trees, walls and hedging which still remain today (Figure 2.4).

In 1653 the Great Walk was built from the courtyard by the house to the boundary line of trees. Although the field north-west of the house was ploughed in the 1970s, the evidence for the line of the Great Walk is in Herbert Andrews' report of his visit to the property in 1909.[24] Andrews could still see the raised turf banks of what he called the 'Long Walk' in the field, and measured it as twenty-seven feet wide, running from a gate in the wall surrounding the old courtyard garden to the north-west boundary of the estate. He also noted that the meadow to the east of the Long Walk was studded with elms, with a 'fine avenue' running due north from the farm buildings. Although his plan (Figure 2.5) is a confusing mix of the early twentieth century and Dury and Andrews' map of Hertfordshire of 1766,[25] Andrews makes an important contribution to the history of Quickswood in his positioning of the Great Walk and the orchard to the east of the farmhouse. The elm avenue is contentious and Andrews' configuration of the house is based on Dury and Andrews' drawing, but the location of the kitchen garden and

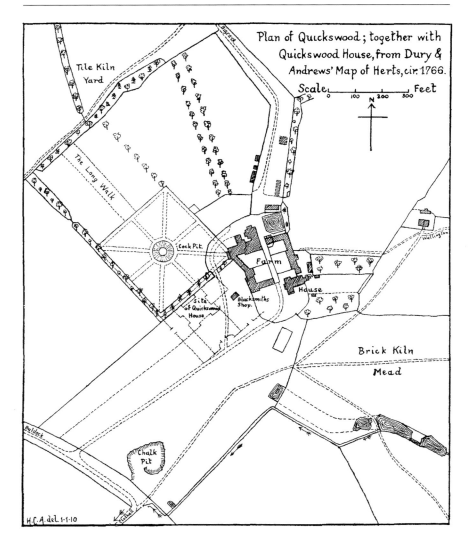

Figure 2.5 Plan of Quickswood by Herbert Andrews, 1910 (not to scale). REPRODUCED BY KIND PERMISSION OF THE EAST HERTS ARCHAEOLOGICAL SOCIETY

orchard is confirmed by parchmarks on a second aerial photograph (Plate 2.2).

Several entries in the accounts provide evidence of the layout of the ornamental gardens to the north of the courtyard garden. In 1638 there is an entry for 'brick dust to mend the walks in the gardens',[26] and in

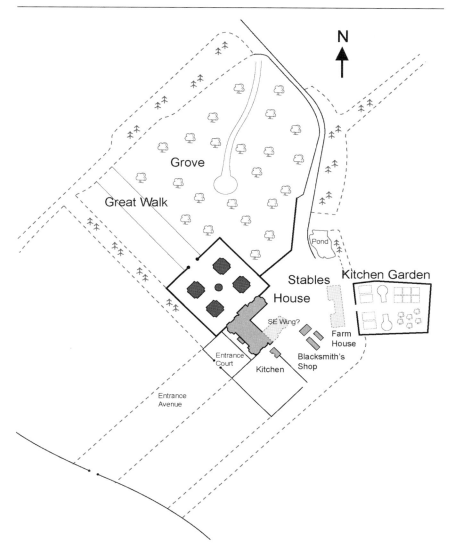

N

Figure 2.6 Sketch plan showing the possible configuration of the house and gardens at Quickswood in the second half of the seventeenth century. © CAROLINE DALTON

1654 an account for 'new laying of walks in the garden'.[27] The Earl paid Mr Banbury £7 for trees in 1655 and purchased laurels in 1656, which suggests that a small woodland or grove was planted at this time.[28] There is no reference to flowers in the accounts. A possible configuration of the courtyard garden, the Great Walk and the grove in the second half of the seventeenth century is illustrated in Figure 2.6. Note that the layout of the courtyard garden is conjecture founded upon the prevailing style.

The accounts continue to paint a vivid picture of life at the second Earl's hunting lodge right up to his death in 1668. It is notable that almost immediately on the accession of William's son James, the third Earl of Salisbury, the expenses for the gardens at Quickswood started to decrease. This almost certainly means that James did not use Quickswood as often as his father, although he and his son (also James) did make occasional trips there. In 1693 there were expenses for the hounds when the fourth Earl 'went to Quixwood to catch foxes'.[29]

Quickswood in the eighteenth century

At the dawn of the eighteenth century James, the fifth Earl, was aged only nine. The hunting lodge at Quickswood must have lain dormant for some years, although repairs and maintenance continued. There were regular payments to the gardeners and records of hedge-cutting, work in the arbour, in the orchard and on the long pond during this period.[30]

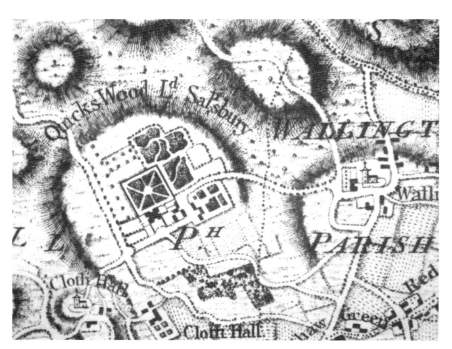

Figure 2.7 Detail of Dury and Andrews' county map, 1766, showing Quickswood.
REPRODUCED BY KIND PERMISSION OF THE HERTFORDSHIRE RECORD SOCIETY

Acknowledgements
I would like to thank Robin Harcourt Williams for access to and permission to reproduce material from the Hatfield House Archive, and for kindly permitting me to draw on and quote from his unpublished 'Notes on the history of Quickswood'. The East Herts Archaeological Society kindly gave me permission to draw on the report by H.C. Andrews and reproduce his plan of Quickswood. Mr Christopher Wilson of Quickswood Farm allowed me access to survey the site and take photographs, and gave me permission to reproduce the aerial photographs. My son, Peter Dalton, digitised my drawing of the seventeenth-century garden at Quickswood.

Notes
1. H.C. Andrews, 'Quickswood, Clothall', *Transactions of the East Herts Archaeological Society,* IV, 1908–9 (1910), p. 94. Andrews was quoting from *Visitations of Hertfordshire,* 1572, Harl. MS., No. 6147.
2. N. Salmon, *The history of Hertfordshire* (London, 1728), p. 332.
3. Andrews, 'Quickswood', p. 95.
4. HHA, catalogue of seventeenth- and eighteenth-century accounts and bills relating to Quickswood.
5. HHA, FP 5/79, 'stone carried for the paving of Quixwood', 1614.
6. Hatfield House website, www.hatfield-house.co.uk/history, accessed 01/12/2005.
7. HHA, CPM Supp. 82, plan by Thomas Heath, *The gallarie at Quexwood,* dated on reverse 1620. Robert Lyminge drew plans for the kitchen which was built in 1623–4.
8. R. Harcourt Williams, 'Notes on the history of Quickswood' (unpublished).
9. *Ibid.*
10. *Ibid.*
11. Science Museum website, www.sciencemuseum.org.uk/on-line/wells-clock, accessed 10/12/2005. Relating to the dating of the Dover Castle Clock: 'The clock is most likely to date from the early 17th century because of its similarity to one from Quickswood Farm in Hertfordshire, which was made in 1625'.
12. HHA, FP 5/157–60, 'The warrener to buy ferrets', 1621.
13. HHA, SFP 2/145, 1661.
14. HHA, Herts 4/07, note of a lease of a brick lime kiln, 1619.
15. D. Jacques and A.J. van der Horst, *The gardens of William and Mary* (London, 1988), p. 150.
16. HHA, SFP 1/207, '220 quinces and portage for Quixwood, osiers, quicksets laths nails and pole for the gardens. 110 elms', 1619.
17. HHA, SFP 1/255 , 'Trees for Quickswood', 1624. Prior to decimalisation, there were 20 shillings (s) to the pound (£) and 12 pennies (d) to the shilling. Therefore a shilling was worth 5p and there were 2.4d to a decimal penny (p).
18. HHA, FP 6/50, 'Cherry, peach and nectarine trees for Hatfield and Quickswood', 1631.
19. HHA, FP 6/50, Bill from John Easden, 1655.
20. HHA, SFP 2/145, 'Making the arbour in the great orchard', 1661.
21. Quickswood survived the Civil War unscathed, largely because William Cecil was a supporter of Parliament, although the accounts record an entry for 'quartering of troops at Quixwood House' in 1647: Harcourt Williams, 'Quickswood'.
22. Andrews, 'Quickswood', p. 97.
23. HHA, FP25 2/238, 'New gate for the walk before the house', 1655.
24. Andrews, 'Quickswood', p. 97.
25. A. Dury and J. Andrews, *A topographical map of Hartford-Shire* (1766; republished by the Hertfordshire Record Society in 2004).
26. HHA, General 4/62, 'Charges for the gardens', 1638.
27. HHA, FP 2/231–6, 'Charges for new laying of walks in the garden', 1654.
28. HHA, FP25 2/238, 'Trees for Quickswood gardens', 1655.
29. *Ibid.*

30. HHA, SFP 3/158, 'cutting the hedge in the orchard', 1706, 'work in the arbour and the garden', 'work in the gardens, orchard and long pond', 1713.
31. Hatfield House website, accessed 01/12/2005.
32. Andrews, 'Quickswood' p. 98.
33. A. Bryant, *The county of Hertford from actual survey* (1822; republished by the Hertfordshire Record Society in 2003).
34. Andrews, 'Quickswood', p. 99.
35. Harcourt Williams, 'Quickswood'.
36. Andrews, 'Quickswood', p. 97.

Bibliography

Primary sources
Bryant, A., *The county of Hertford from actual survey* (1822; republished by the Hertfordshire Record Society in 2003)
Digimap Historic, www.digimap.edina.ac.uk, 1883–1892, accessed 10/12/2005
Dury, A. and Andrews, J., *A topographical map of Hartford-Shire* (1766; republished by the Hertfordshire Record Society in 2004)
Edina Digimap, www.digimap.edina.ac.uk, 2005, accessed 10/12/2005
Hatfield House Archive (hereafter HHA), aerial photographs in the Quickswood Private Collection *c.*2003 (copyright C. Wilson)
HHA, catalogue of seventeenth- and eighteenth-century accounts and bills relating to Quickswood, unpublished (copyright The Marquess of Salisbury)
HHA, CPM Supp. 82, plan by Thomas Heath, 1620, showing 'How the gallarie at Quixwood may be divided into chambers and other rooms' (copyright The Marquess of Salisbury)

Secondary sources
Andrews, H.C., 'Quickswood, Clothall', *Transactions of the East Herts Archaeological Society*, IV, 1908–9 (1910)
Harcourt Williams, R., 'Notes on the history of Quickswood' (unpublished)
Jacques, D. and van der Horst, A.J., *The gardens of William and Mary* (London, 1988)
Salmon, N., *The history of Hertfordshire* (London, 1728)

Websites
Hatfield House website, **www.hatfield-house.co.uk/history** (accessed 01/12/2005)
Science Museum web pages, **www.sciencemuseum.org.uk/on-line/wells-clock** (accessed 10/12/2005)

CHAPTER THREE

Charles Bridgeman at Tring Park: a reassessment

Alan Fletcher

Figure 3.1 Tring Park by John Oliver for Sir Henry Chauncy's *The historical antiquities of Hertfordshire*, 1700. REPRODUCED BY KIND PERMISSION OF HALS

Henry Guy was one of the Grooms of the Bedchamber of Charles II and held other important posts; in 1673 he was deputy steward of the Manor of Tring and in 1679 he became lord of the Manor. At some time in the 1680s he had a house, Tring Manor, built for him by Sir Christopher Wren; an engraving of the south (garden) front of the house, dedicated by John Oliver to Henry Guy, appears in Chauncy, *The historical antiquities of Hertfordshire*, 1700[1] (Figure 3.1), and there is a description and plan of the accommodation in *English houses 1200–1800. The Hertfordshire evidence;*[2] it was a 'triple-pile' nine-bay, two-storey house, with attic and basement, and had a lawn in front of it. There is a tradition that Nell Gwynne stayed in the house.

In 1705 Henry Guy sold his estate to Sir William Gore, a former Lord Mayor of London.[3] Sir William died in January 1708 and he was succeeded by his eldest son, William Gore, who lived in the house until his death in 1739.

There are two plans of the formal gardens as they existed in the first half of the eighteenth century: an estate map of Tring surveyed by John Colbeck for William Gore in 1719 (Plate 3.1); and Badeslade's engraving of 1739 in *Vitruvius Britannicus* IV (Figure 3.2). The estate map may have been drawn a few years later than 1719,[4] and the engraving may have been drawn a few years before it was published. Both the map and the engraving show a series of gardens stretching for a long way east from the lawn in front of the house – elaborate parterres, a formal pool with a fountain and an orangery fronting it, more parterres, a bowling green overlooked by a pavilion with a conical dome and then formal hedged enclosures and an alcove at the far end; to the west of the lawn there is a small formal garden and a pavilion backing on to the kitchen garden.

To the south is a long canal with two flanking rows of trees on each side, and then a series of terraces surmounted by a large pyramid. Colbeck's estate map shows the whole of the park, which rises up to the wooded Chilterns escarpment; there are several avenues and formal clumps of trees, while in the south-eastern corner there is a wood with rides cut into it and an obelisk and summerhouse at focal points. The engraving does not show the whole park, but what it does show is similar to that shown on the map. On the north side of the house both map and engraving show a wide avenue with a pool in the middle going down to the public road in the town.

Hitherto the generally accepted view has been that the landscape gardener Charles Bridgeman and the architect James Gibbs combined in the 1720s to create all the formal gardens and the works in the park.[5] I am of the opinion, however, that Bridgeman and Gibbs were only responsible for the works going south into the park – the canal, avenues, pyramid, woodland rides, obelisk and summerhouse – and probably the so-called 'Nell Gwynne' avenue to the north: the long east–west line of

Notes

1. H. Chauncy, *The historical antiquities of Hertfordshire* (London, 1700), pp. 592–3.
2. J.T. Smith, *English houses 1200–1800. The Hertfordshire evidence* (London, 1992), p. 84.
3. J.E. Cussans, *History of Hertfordshire* (1870–81) and A.A. Hanham, 'Guy, Henry (*bap.* 1631, *d.* 1711)', *Oxford Dictionary of National Biography* (Oxford, 2004), www.oxforddnb.com/view/article/11798/2004-09, accessed 18 Jan 2007 as archived article (no longer current version), give 1702 as the date when Henry Guy sold the estate to Sir William Gore, but I cannot find any contemporary evidence to support this. It is established that the Lordship of the Manor was conveyed to Sir William at Michaelmas 1705 (Victoria County History citing Feet of Fines, 4 Queen Anne). I think it reasonable to assume that the estate was sold at the same time, which is also the time when Guy retired from Parliament.
4. The estate map was owned by Dr Miriam Rothschild and there is a colour illustration of it in her book, *The Rothschild gardens* (London, 1996), pp. 150–1. The map may have been drawn rather later than 1719, as it is part of a series covering all William Gore's estate and, although based on Colbeck's survey, many of them bear the signature *'Johann Smith fecit'*: in one case this is followed by the date 1730.
5. For example, G. Jackson-Stops, *Country Life,* 187, 25 November 1993, pp. 60–3.
6. HALS, QS/B/7, 1711, p. 105.
7. HALS, J. Oliver, *The actual survey of the county of Hertford* (1695).
8. In my opinion Henry Guy laid out the east–west gardens between 1695 and 1705. In 1695 he resigned from the Treasury in disgrace but he was only in the Tower for a short time; he was still very wealthy and he had enough energy left to re-enter Parliament in 1702.
9. Yorkshire Archaeological Society, MS 328, anonymous journal entitled 'Account of my Journey begun 6 Augt. 1724'.
10. G. Jackson-Stops, 'Tring Park, Hertfordshire', *Country Life,* 187, 25 November 1993, pp. 60–3; P. Willis, *Charles Bridgeman and the English landscape garden* (London, 1977), p. 184.
11. G. Jackson-Stops, 'Tring Park, Hertfordshire', *Country Life,* 187, 25 November 1993, pp. 60–3.
12. H. Walpole, *Anecdotes of painting in England,* IV (London, 1782), p. 286.
13. H. Colvin, *A bibliographic dictionary of British architects 1600–1840* (London, 1978), p. 343.
14. HALS, DP/111/26/2, Tring Parish Enclosure map, 1799.

Bibliography

Primary sources
Bodleian Library, Oxford, Gough collection, MSGD a4 fo.32, plan of Tring Park by
    Charles Bridgeman
Hertfordshire Archives and Local Studies (hereafter HALS), DP/111/26/2, Tring Parish
    Enclosure map, 1799
HALS, Dury, A. and Andrews J., *A topographical map of Hartford-Shire* (1766; republished by
    the Hertfordshire Record Society in 2004)
HALS, Oliver, J., *The actual survey of the county of Hertford* (1695); republished in Hodson, D.,
    Four County Maps of Hertfordshire (Stevenage, 1985)
HALS, QS/B/7, Quarter Session Books for 1711
Yorkshire Archaeological Society, MS 328, anonymous journal entitled 'Account of my Journey
    begun 6 Augt. 1724'

Secondary sources
Campbell, C., *Vitruvius Britannicus* (London, 1739)
Chauncy, H., *The historical antiquities of Hertfordshire* (London, 1700)
Colvin, H., *A bibliographic dictionary of British architects 1600–1840* (London, 1978)
Cussans, J.E., *History of Hertfordshire* (1870–81)
Jackson-Stops, G., 'Tring Park, Hertfordshire', *Country Life,* 187, 25 November 1993
Rothschild, M., *The Rothschild gardens* (London, 1996)
Salmon, N., *The history of Hertfordshire* (London, 1728)
Smith, J.T., *English houses 1200–1800. The Hertfordshire evidence* (London, 1992)
Walpole, H., *Anecdotes of painting in England,* IV (London, 1782)
Willis, P., *Charles Bridgeman and the English landscape garden* (London, 1977)

Websites
Oxford Dictionary of National Biography website, **www.oxforddnb.com**
    (accessed 18/01/2007)

CHAPTER FOUR

Some Hertfordshire nabobs

Kate Harwood

Estates are landscapes, gaz'd upon a while
Then advertis'd, and auctioneer'd away
W. Cowper, *The Task, Book III* (1785)

Figure 4.1 Map of Hertfordshire estates with East India Company connections. Also shown are the turnpike roads created during the eighteenth century (after T. Rook, *A history of Hertfordshire* [Chichester, 1984] p. 83). © KATE HARWOOD AND ANNE ROWE

Hertfordshire's estates were generally not large but were conveniently close to London, which made them popular with merchants, lawyers and Company men. Over the long eighteenth century directors and governors of the East India Company bought estates in Hertfordshire[1] and spent their Company fortunes on their houses, pleasure grounds, woods and agricultural lands. Some of these *nouveau riche* 'nabobs'[2] handed their estates down to their heirs for a generation or two, but some lost their fortunes even faster than they had made them and their estates were sold (Figure 4.1).

The East India Company, although latterly the quasi-government Civil Service in India and the East Indies, started life as a trading company. It received its Charter on 31 December 1600, after a long period of lobbying by merchants with their eye on the spice trade. This was not the start of the English merchants' attempts to muscle in on the spice trade, but one of its more successful punctuation points. Things did not progress smoothly, with the English ships having to lurk behind

Figure 4.2 The Temple of Suriya at Sezincote, Gloucestershire, with grottoes and waterwheel.
PHOTOGRAPH BY KATE HARWOOD, 2004

islands and waylay homeward-bound Dutch merchantmen. This government-sanctioned piracy was intermittently successful, as when Captain James Lancaster captured a cargo of pepper worth a million pounds.[3] The English set up their first factory at Surat, north of Bombay, in 1608 and from then on visits into the country for trading, botanical forays, exploration and missionary activity provided reports, paintings, drawings and artefacts to be sent back to England to fuel the fashion for the exotic.

The architecture, gardens and landscape of the sub-continent proved irresistible and artists such as William Hodges and the Daniels (uncle and nephew) sent back pictures of the 'pagothas',[4] huts, tombs, forts and palaces. Quite a few old India hands built themselves a temple or two in their gardens back home, although none went so far as Charles Cockerell, at Sezincote in Gloucestershire, with an Indianised house and gardens full of temples and nandi, lotus leaves and elephants (Figure 4.2).

As the eighteenth century progressed the opportunities for making fortunes increased. A stint in India became a well-known route for impoverished younger sons, or members of the trading classes, up the social ladder. Later, the 'Fishing Fleet' would take out young ladies looking for suitable husbands; the unsuccessful ones were 'returned empties'.

Serving in India was seen in some ways as a prison sentence, ameliorated by the vast fortunes to be made.[5] A writer (most junior of the Company's employees) wrote, as he sailed for Calcutta in 1752, 'I do expect it to be of fifteen or twenty years at least. In that time I may be made Governour. If not that, I may make a fortune which will make me live like a gentleman'.[6] There were provisos: mortality from disease and hostilities between the various national Houses – Dutch, Portuguese and French as well as English – made leaving India at the end of one's time uncertain, even before facing the perilous sea crossing of several months. And Bengal was an expensive place to live; in 1754 it was said to be double the price that it was at home.[7]

In 1674 the rules on Private Trade were introduced and, although the Company reserved some commodities to itself, ex-employees still in India could carry on trading through the factories, and ship owners could carry other cargoes. Goods traded were luxurious – gems, gold textiles, ambergris, musk. Fortunes were made.[8]

John Fergusson's Indian fortune was 'honestly acquired' before his return to Stanmore, Middlesex, in 1789 with a gift from grateful Indians of Buddhist sculptures, for which he built a temple surrounded with Indian plants.[9] Another free trader, James Prinsep, came home with £40,000.[10] Prime Minister William Pitt's great-grandfather, Thomas Pitt, who had made and spent one fortune before he returned to Madras to make another as Governor, was also deemed to have made the family's fortune honestly.[11] Lord Clive told his wife he hoped to see all of his friends 'return home with £40 or 50,000' – and George Vansittart, the Governor's younger brother, felt he needed £50,000 and, in 1774, advised his nephew to 'stay for £60,000'.[12] After 1757 the taking of 'presents' and the practice of free trading, while also employed as a factor by the Company, meant that this money came to be seen in England as tainted and its owners as corrupt. This was especially so after Pitt's 1784 India Act and Warren Hastings' impeachment.[13] This did not prevent men from acquiring, and sending back to England, as much money as they could. It did, however, suppress the flamboyant expression of the source.

One of the recognised ways of buying into the Establishment was going into politics, which many did in a local way, becoming high sheriffs or lord lieutenants of their counties. Many became MPs, often for rotten boroughs, and a few, such as the Pitts, founded political dynasties. Another way was to buy estates, particularly if they were close to centres of population – and especially London. Hertfordshire, Essex, Surrey and Middlesex were all popular destinations.

In Hertfordshire, Humphry Repton commented, 'There are few counties in England which possess more natural beauties than Hartfordshire; yet there is none in which those beauties require to be more brought to notice by the assistance of art'.[14] Many eminent landscape designers, before and since Repton, have worked to develop the county's natural beauties, often at the request of wealthy Company men. Two of its grandest landscapes, for example, were laid out for Company men by Charles Bridgeman: Sacombe Park, north of Ware, and Gobions (Gubbins), north of Potters Bar.

Thomas Rolt had started out as a writer in India in 1658, rising to become 'Agent of Persia and President of India' (actually of Surat, the foremost Company factory at that time).[15] He bought Sacombe Park in 1688, enlarged the park and stocked it with deer.[16] His son, Edward, inherited in 1710 and commissioned James Gibbs to design a house; Gibbs' design was never executed, although he did publish the plans in his *Book of architecture*.[17] A plan by Bridgeman exists in the Bodleian

Library for a design for the garden (see Plate 4.1).[18] This is a very interesting bastion-shaped layout, perhaps reflecting the forts by Vauban which would have been familiar from the Duke of Marlborough's European campaigns, and which was repeated at other Bridgeman gardens, such as Grimsthorpe in Lincolnshire.

The walled kitchen garden, with massive gates and buttresses, was designed by Vanbrugh,[19] who had also served the Company in Surat for fifteen months from 1683 as a factor, which entailed travelling within India trading textiles.[20] He would have seen the massive walls surrounding the city states and, given Rolt's India connections, such a reference would have been appropriate.[21] Sir Matthew Decker described the walls of the Sacombe kitchen garden as 'so strongly built by Van Brock [sic], as if they were to defend a Citty [sic]'.[22] It was gardening on the grand scale, with a formal bason and parterre and vistas through blocks of densely planted woodland leading to rond-points, a cascade and a long canal and bason. The amphitheatre was designed with four earth banks, but appears not to have been completed as there is no remaining contemporary planting, as there is elsewhere. Whether the parterre was completed before the death of Edward Rolt *c.* 1722 is not clear. However, the landscape was well known for its painterly qualities; in 1728 Salmon wrote:

> it's hard to say whether Nature or Art be most admirable here. The Artist seems to have attempted shewing Nature to its greatest advantage. At the end of one Walk is a sort of Theatrical Work, shaded by Oaks at unequal Distances, as they happened to grow, such as one would wish represented in a Landschape.[23]

An intimation of the magnificence of Sacombe can be gained from the descriptions of Gobions, another early eighteenth-century garden.

Gobions, or Gubbins, was purchased in 1709 by Jeremy Sambrooke, who had inherited his money from his grandfather, Samuel, 'writer of the Company's letters and Keeper of the Callicoe warehouse'.[24] Both his father and brother followed the (new) family tradition of becoming nabobs, but Jeremy stayed at home and spent his fortune on the pleasure grounds described by Daniel Defoe as 'one of the most remarkable curiosities in England'.[25] He commissioned James Gibbs and Charles Bridgeman to lay out these grounds. Bridgeman's design[26] of formal gardens, canal, bowling green and so forth was complemented by a range of buildings by Gibbs. These included a dovecote and a temple to

Figure 4.3 The archway in Gobions Park from the south, with the mansion in the distance, by Buckler, 1840. REPRODUCED BY KIND PERMISSION OF HALS (KNOWSLEY CLUTTERBUCK 4, p. 448B)

Figure 4.4 'A perspective view of the Bowling Green &c at Gubbins in Hertfordshire, a seat of Sir Jeremy Sambrooke, Bart.', drawn by Chatelain. REPRODUCED BY KIND PERMISSION OF HALS (KNOWSLEY CLUTTERBUCK 4, p. 452A)

overlook the bowling green. The mock-medieval folly arch overlooking the whole and dominating the skyline may also have been by Gibbs (Figures 4.3 and 4.4).

A slightly later description explains why 'Her Majesty [Queen Caroline], with the three eldest Princesses, visited … [and] viewed his fine gardens, waterworks and his collection of curiosities' in July 1732:[27]

> Imagine to yourself a vast Hill, shaded all over with a Forest of Oaks, through which have been cut an infinite Number of Alleys covered with the finest Gravel … a large Square, embellished with Orange-trees and Statues, and with a beautiful Summerhouse, whose Windows present on every Side a most delicious Prospect … a magnificent Bason, adorned with green Pyramids, orange-trees, Statues, and surrounded with wide-extending alleys; and then you see a kind of verdant Circle, all covered with the Trees of the Forest, but illumined with so much Art and Taste, as to fill the Eye with Raptures. In short, the Beauty of the Alleys, whose verdant Hedges are of a surprising Height, the pleasing Variety of the Prospects, the Richness of the Ornaments, the singular Taste that prevails through the Whole Distribution, and the Choice of the different Parts of this charming Place, form all together almost the only Garden of its kind.[28]

The writer, George Bickham (the Younger), sees in it 'a sensible Resemblance to *Stow*', although 'Notwithstanding all the surprising Greatness of *Gubbins* still it must submit to *Stow*', but it still 'deserves a Traveller's Admiration'.[29]

After Sambrooke's death in 1754, the estate eventually passed to a Company deputy director, John Hunter, a former free merchant in Bombay who had made a fortune of upwards of £100,000[30] by 'long success in trade'. Hunter enlarged the estate partly by enclosing part of North Mymms Common. He willed Gobions to Thomas Hunter (né Holmes), a 'gentleman high in the Company's service in Bombay', who had married the Governor Hornby's daughter.[31] Thomas Hunter subsequently sold the estate in 1815.

The grounds had been maintained as in Sambrooke's time and a description of the garden tour, published in 1774 in *The Ambulator*,[32] probably comes from William Toldervy's account in his letters of 1762.[33] Toldervy started his visit in the wilderness on the

> delightful path, which conducted me into a charming Wood. This Walk is irregularly cut through the Underwood, but the lofty Oaks which overshadow it

are not disturbed. [Shortly afterwards, I] suddenly came into the most ravishing Spot that can be imagined. It is a perfect Rotunda, about the same Diameter with the Ring in Hyde Park. Here the Underwood is entirely taken away, but the Oak trees, which are very strait, and vastly high, remain entire. They are a great many, and the Ground between them is entirely covered with a thick, short Moss of the Colour of Gold. The whole is surrounded by a Gravel Walk, about eight Feet wide. On one Side is a large Alcove … Opposite to the Place of my Entrance … is another Avenue, which brought me to a large Alcove, situate at the End of an oblong Piece of Water; on each Side of whose Banks are fine Gravel Walks, lined with Rows of Trees. This pond is so formed that a Part of it is deep, and therefore the Bottom not easily seen; but the other Part is shallow … The Grass at the Bottom, when covered with Water, hath a sweet Effect. [From the alcove] I had a View over the Water to a fine large figure of Time … holding a large Sun-Dial … beyond whom, through a Vista, the Eye is infallibly led to an Obelisk, at a considerable Distance, beyond the Gardens.

[From the Mansion House,] which did not excite my Curiosity, [I] was conducted by one of the Gardeners through a most superb and elegant Walk, which terminated at a Summer-House, built of Wood in the Lattice Manner, and painted green. We then turned to the Left, through meandering Walks … to a very affecting Grotto; which having passed, a large Arch presented itself across the Walk, and through that I beheld a most ravishing Cascade … Continuing … I turned to the Right … to a Seat, where the Cascade has a more distant Sound. This is a very contemplative Situation … From the last mentioned Seat a pretty Walk brought me to a good statue of Hercules … from whence, through a verdant Arch, appears a beautiful Canal; at the End of which is a handsome Temple, whose Front is supported by four Pillars. In this Temple are two Bustoes of … Madam Sambrooke and Madam Betty …

On one Side of the Canal is a Roman Gladiator … Leaving this Canal, I ascended a strait Walk, which brought me, on the Left-Hand, to a Cleopatra, as stung with an Asp. This Figure stands upon a Pedestal, in a Meadow, at some Distance; and, on our Right, appeared a very large and beautiful Urn. The Top of our Walk terminated at a large Oak, from whence there is a View over the Canal … to the Gladiator; and from thence, through a Grove, to a lofty Pigeon-House. Turning to our Right, we came to the neatest and most retired Bowling-Green I ever saw; at one End of which, is the Urn before mentioned, and at the other a Summer-House, full of Orange and Lemon-Trees, with fine Fruit upon them. On one Side of the Green is a Statue of Venus, and on the other, one of Adonis.

No wonder that Horace Walpole could say, in his influential *History of the modern taste in gardening,* that he had 'many detached thoughts, that strongly indicated the dawn of modern taste'.[34]

The end of the era came with a further sale of the Gobions estate in 1838. The hyperbolic sales particulars include a description of the

> MAGNIFICENT PARK of 328 acres chiefly rich meadow land, Embellished with Stately Avenues, Groves and woods of the Finest Timber, a Triumphal Arch commemorative of Queen Elizabeth's progress in 1560, Pleasure Grounds, Lawns, Shrubberies, Gardens, Conservatories, A Splendid lake, fishing temple, canal, ice house, ornamental Lodges, and other decorations of a superior order, Commanding a Finely Elevated and picturesque situation, only Sixteen Miles from London, in the much admired COUNTY OF HERTFORD, Within a short Drive of Hatfield House, and other distinguished Residences of the Aristocracy.[35]

But the vast amount of money needed to develop and sustain this garden for nearly 100 years had come from the Company and from India.

Charles Bridgeman also laid out the gardens of Moor Park, Rickmansworth, c.1720–28, not for an East India Company man but for South Sea Company man, Benjamin Styles. Here the serpentine walks and temples in woodland with turfed ramps and terraces, as at Gobions, sat in a formal landscape with the usual long canal and bason, rond-points and rides.[36] In 1750 the landscape of Moor Park was remodelled by 'Capability' Brown and it was this that was purchased by Thomas Bates Rous (c.1739–99), a director of the East India Company for twenty-four years between 1773 and 1799.[37]

Rous had started out as the commander of the East Indiaman *Britannia* in 1762 and, on inheriting money from his father in 1771, he spent £10,000 winning the parliamentary seat for Worcester, but was unseated after being found guilty of bribery. He purchased Moor Park in 1785 and proceeded to demolish the wings of the house, which had been connected by colonnades to the main block,[38] in order to raise money from the sale of the materials – possibly because his funds were depleted by fighting four elections in ten years (Figure 4.5).

Muffets (formerly Nashes Farm), a near neighbour of Gobions, was owned by John Michie (n.d.–1788), a Company director, on and off, from 1770 to 1783 as well as a navy agent and wine merchant. Returning to England possessed of a 'good moderate fortune'[39] he purchased the estate, after first leasing it, in 1776.[40] He augmented his property in 1782 by purchasing part of Bradmore Farm and acquiring the copyhold of the manor of Brookmans from Sir Charles Cocks of

Brookmans Park.[41] He was provided with further India connections by his nephew, Jonathan Duncan, who was Governor of Bombay from 1794 to 1811. Like Rous, he spent his later years in straitened circumstances, complaining of financial hardship and preferring to 'live very private in the Country'.[42]

Thomas Rumbold (1736–91) rose from humble beginnings; his father, William, was a purser on the East Indiaman *King George*. Thomas started out as a writer in Madras in 1752 but entered the army and fought at Trichinopoly (1754)[43] and Plassey (1757).[44] With two partners he administered the Company revenue at Chittagong and made enough money to own several ships and his own shipyard at Barkarganj.[45] Other profitable ventures ensued and he returned home with a fortune of £200,000–300,000. He returned to India in 1778 to become Governor of Madras (until 1781) but was recalled in disgrace, his assets frozen for 'certain breaches of Public Trust and High Crimes and Misdemeanours,[46] committed by them [he had a partner in crime] while they respectively held the offices of Governor and President ... of Fort St George [Madras] on the coast of Coromandel in the East Indies'.[47] He was sued by the Company for £1,000,000. He subsequently escaped punishment but it

Figure 4.5 Moor Park, by H.G. Oldfield, *c.*1800. REPRODUCED BY KIND PERMISSION OF HALS (OLDFIELD DRAWINGS 5, p. 385)

was suggested that the action had been 'compromised, doubtless for a satisfactory consideration' and it was well known that he was 'one of the most notorious nabobs of his time'.[48]

Rumbold bought Woodhall Park at Watton-at-Stone in 1774 by a convoluted process from one of his erstwhile partners at Chittagong, Henry Verelst, now Governor of Bengal, with a mortgage provided by Verelst and Lord Clive of India. Formerly the property of the Boteler family, this 'fine estate' contained a complex of formal gardens around the house, with avenues to the south-east and south-west. It was situated on a rise above the River Beane, which flowed round the park (Figure 4.6). Rumbold commissioned Thomas Leverton in 1777 to build a new mansion further north in the park,[49] while he disappeared back to India again, which caused considerable problems both for Leverton and for Rumbold's attorneys. By the time of Rumbold's death in 1791, the garden was said to boast 'a greater profusion of hot walls and forcing-fruit houses than perhaps any garden in the kingdom'.[50]

Although Rumbold left his estate to his family, by a complicated will which pleased no one, Woodhall Park was acquired in 1797 by Paul Benfield (1741–1810), whose financial dealings were on a par with

Figure 4.6 'Park at Woodhall Park, Seat of John Abel Smith', by Buckler, 1834. REPRODUCED BY KIND PERMISSION OF HALS (KNOWSLEY CLUTTERBUCK 7, p. 474C)

Rumbold's.[51] He and Rumbold had corresponded over East India affairs and Benfield had even been appointed in Rumbold's place while the alleged misdemeanours of Madras were being investigated.[52] Edmund Burke had waged a long campaign over the corruption in the Company and his speech regarding the debts of the Nawab of the Carnatic included an attack on Benfield in which he denounced him as 'a criminal who long since ought to have fattened the region's kites with his offal'.[53] Benfield had started in India in 1764 and had amassed a fortune of over £500,000, but managed to lose it all speculating.[54] Part of his speculation was dealing in Hertfordshire estates. He was involved with Gobions, Landvers, Whempstead, Watkins Hall, Clay Hill, and the manors of Bardolph, Aston, Crowbury and Patchendon, and settled an estate of £4,000 *per annum* on his son.[55] Benfield had also been suspended in disgrace by the Company, in 1781, and subsequently reinstated.[56]

Jacob Bosanquet (*c*.1756–1828) bought Broxbournebury (Figure 4.7) for £30,250, a reduction from the asking price of £30,800, from Lord Monson in 1789. He was a Company director for many years between 1782 and 1827, Chairman of Directors between 1799 and 1812, and a partner in Bosanquet and Willerman, silk merchants of

Figure 4.7 View of Broxbournebury, by H.G. Oldfield, c.1800. REPRODUCED BY KIND PERMISSION OF HALS (OLDFIELD DRAWINGS 1, p. 412)

Throgmorton Street. No evidence has been found to suggest he made his fortune by going to India, but he did have property in the West Indies. He was not universally popular, being dubbed by the then President of the Board of Control in 1802 a 'great coxcomb and among the least pleasant man [sic] to act with that have fallen my way'.[57]

The park at Broxbournebury had been in existence since 1670 and, when Bosanquet bought the estate, the gardens were elaborate but run down. Situated on a slight rise, the house had formal gardens and a canal flanked by avenues running north-west of the mansion, and avenues along the south-east entrance drive. It was said that the Monsons had removed £20,000 of oak in the years before they left. Bosanquet replanted, especially along White Stubbs Lane and Pembury Lane. He also extended the estate with the purchase of the manors of Hoddesdonbury and Baas.[58]

Edward Harrison (?–1725) had inherited Balls Park (Figure 4.8) in 1725 from his father Richard. The house had been built about 1640 by Sir John Harrison, Edward's grandfather and a noted Royalist, and was of enormous architectural importance in Hertfordshire. Edward had started out in 1703 as captain of the *Kent,* an East Indiaman on the

Figure 4.8 Gate to formal gardens at Balls Park, Hertford, with Edward Harrison's monogram.
PHOTOGRAPH BY KATE HARWOOD, 2006

Canton run.[59] He was appointed President and Governor of Fort St George (Madras) in 1711[60] and became a Company director, serving as chairman twice. Unusually, he seems to have 'acquired a large fortune with a very fair character'[61] after a somewhat shaky start in 1695, when he fought a duel in the French padre's garden and was fined five pagodas.[62] His father having improved the mansion, Edward Harrison set about the grounds.

He laid out avenues north, east and west of the house and an oblique one north-west towards Hertford. He also laid out a canal fifty yards long, with a circular bason at the end, due south of the house. The canal was flanked by a wilderness with paths through the shrubs and, at the far end, a further avenue, flanked at its furthest end by blocks of woodland, reached out to the boundary of the pleasure grounds.[63] Harrison also extended the estate with the purchase of the manor of Datchworth and of Smith's Farm.

At about the same time, in 1728, John Deane, Company director, bought Little Grove at Barnet before moving on to Wormleybury in 1733, where he rebuilt the mansion to the designs of Robert Mylne (of Little Amwell). Wormleybury garden was probably laid out by Deane's

Figure 4.9 Sandridge Lodge, by H.G. Oldfield, *c.*1798. REPRODUCED BY KIND PERMISSION OF HALS (OLDFIELD DRAWINGS 8, p. 549)

successor, Alexander Hume, another Company director.[64] It incorporated straight walks, yew hedges and a canal with a circular basin, subsequently altered to a crescent-shaped lake. Robert Adam was consulted over plans for garden buildings (see Plate 4.2).[65]

The house had a formal approach, with a walled garden to one side, and the forecourt walls were covered with nearly 100 trees of choice varieties of apricots, peaches, cherries and other fruits. A wilderness lay beyond the walled garden. Alexander and his successor, his brother Abraham, planted oriental planes, cedars of Lebanon, lombardy poplars, swamp cypress, *Ginkgo biloba* and *Magnolia demidata* (now *conspicua*) in the grounds.

Charles Bourchier of Tyttenhanger was another serial buyer of Hertfordshire estates. He was also Governor of Madras for the Company from 1767 to 1770, having first been granted a Company commission in 1768.[66] He purchased Marshalswick, near St Albans, in 1788. Bourchier added a west wing to the house, extended the estate and changed its name to 'Sandridge Lodge'. By 1799 the house and gardens had 75 acres of estate associated with it. Marshalls Wick Farm had another 120 acres, in addition to the garden and orchard.[67]

The Oldfield illustration of Sandridge Lodge (1798; Figure 4.9) and a watercolour painting of the house (*c*.1825)[68] both indicate that a formal garden was no longer in front of the house as it had been in 1766 (Dury and Andrews). Bourchier sold the estate on in 1802. Meanwhile, he had purchased Colney Park House, now All Saints Pastoral Centre, at London Colney.

Wall Hall, Aldenham, was bought for £24,000 in 1799 by George Woodford Thellusson, director of the Company from 1799 to 1807 and banker to the Company. He was obviously a man of some renown, upon whom Dickens based his man of probity, Jarvis Lorrie, the Tellson's Bank representative in *A Tale of Two Cities*. Thellusson purchased 'a very large farm' with the fortune made from the Company and proceeded to establish a gentleman's estate.[69] The result was a gothicised mansion, later named 'Aldenham Abbey', built to the north of the old farm and completed in 1802. Some detailing in the house was done by Sir John Soane in 1801,[70] and Humphry Repton was called on for advice on the landscape, producing a 'Red Book' after a visit in 1802.[71] This proposed a new drive, new buildings (some still existing) and the opening up of some vistas, including one towards the church.

The Sale Map of 1812 (Figure 4.10) shows that farmland has made way for formal gardens, groves, plantations, lawns, shrubberies and an icehouse, as well as a mock ruin of brick rendered with cement in the picturesque Gothic style.[72] A new south drive curves through the landscape from the new lodges in Aldenham and a 'sunk fence' separates the west lawns from a right of way, permitting uninterrupted views towards Watford. It is not possible to say how much of this was Repton's work, as the map for the Red Book does not survive. Certainly, not all of Repton's suggestions appear to have been executed but the extent of the work, not all of it suggested in the Red Book, may indicate that further advice was sought by Thellusson, from Repton or from someone else. The trellis bridge carrying the 'high road' over the proposed drive, for example, does not appear on the 1812 map and, indeed, the drive does not follow Repton's suggested route. Following Thellusson's death in 1812 the 230-acre estate was sold at auction and the particulars detail 'the beautiful pleasure grounds, plantations [and] gardens'. There were also 'Two capital Kitchen gardens, a noble circular-fronted peach-house with graperies at the ends, melon ground, orchard, [and] shrubbery walks leading through the Gothic Ruins to a spacious Rustic Dairy'. In addition to a herb garden and an orchard, there was a large icehouse and pheasantry, a trellis-fronted poultry-house and a 'circular conservatory with Rustic Virandas entwined by Honeysuckle … [which led] to an extensive range of Pheasantries, Aviaries, Bowers, &c'.[73]

Thellusson was instrumental in setting up the East India College at Haileybury, Hertford Heath, for the education of the Company officials. The college had opened in Hertford Castle in 1806 as a temporary measure and William Wilkins was called in to design new premises round a quadrangle, reminiscent of the Oxbridge colleges. The site chosen was Hailey (Bury) House, which had been purchased at auction in 1805.[74] Repton, an old friend of Wilkins's, visited Haileybury twice in November 1808 and drew up a plan, but the only record of his work here is a sketch map showing the combining of three old brick pits into two sinuous pools. The addition of a carefully sited island and some skilful planting gave the impression that this was a meandering river (Plate 4.3).[75]

Thomas Barr of Balls Pond Nursery, Islington, submitted an estimate of £1,350 for carrying out the work, which was paid in instalments. The site was levelled and new roads laid. An avenue of 420 horse chestnuts ('good healthy trees from 11 to 12 feet high') and tree and shrub

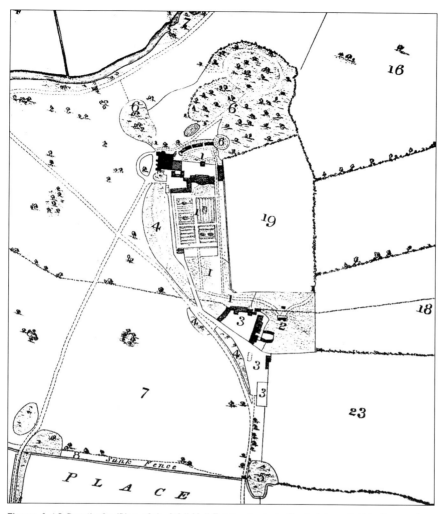

Figure 4.10 Detail of a 'Plan of the Wall Hall Estate situate in the Parishes of Aldenham and Saint Stephens in the County of Herts 1812', by John Shaw. REPRODUCED BY KIND PERMISSION OF HALS (DP/3/29/9B)

plantations were laid out and Repton designed a terrace to link the south side of the building to the grounds.[76]

Haileybury had many staff from India,[77] not only professors of the Indian languages but also domestic and ancillary staff, many of whom married and settled in the locality. One such was the college butler, Peter Cleophas, who built the Havelock Arms and Hailey Lodge. The first 'Chinese' wisteria in England was reputed to have been planted at

Haileybury, as well as a number of unusual trees of Eastern origin in the Trevelyan House and the Master's House gardens.[78] The importance of the college was severely compromised, however, when the 1853 Government of India Act introduced the power to examine candidates for direct appointments without attendance at Haileybury. There were no more admissions after January 1856 and the college closed on 31 January 1858, the year that the Company was forced to wind up by the government.

Another 'wealthy banker' was John Dorrien (*c.*1714–1784) of Berkhamsted, who was director of the Company between 1755 and 1763. Either he or his son, Thomas, acquired Haresfoot, near Berkhamsted. John Dorrien was among those Company men who were pricked for Sheriff of Hertfordshire; he served in 1773.

Laurence Sullivan (*c.*1713–1786) was also a director of the Company, on and off, for forty-one years until his death. He was another social climber who started as a factor in Bombay in 1740 and rose to Council status before leaving with a modest fortune in 1753.[79] He purchased Ponsbourne Park in 1761 for £13,000 and, 'finding the manor house in decay, decided on pulling it down, and built the present mansion in the centre of the estate'[80] (this is not the mansion which survives today). By 1764 he had built not only the mansion but a cottage, a dove house and two gardens, within nine acres of land.[81] Remains of these gardens were seen by the East Herts Archaeological Society on their visit to Ponsbourne in 1907, although they did not describe them.[82]

These, then, were some of the men who made their money in the Company and spent it buying or improving their Hertfordshire estates. But the influence of plants from the Indian sub-continent on the landscape was, and is, arguably greater, although less dramatic a feature than temples and canals. Plants from south-east Asia have been known since medieval times, although early arrivals, such as common purslane (*Portulaca oleracea*) probably came via Turkey or the Levant. By the eighteenth century the Company was shipping vast quantities of seeds and seedlings from India, China and the East Indies, to feed the growing network of plant enthusiasts who raised and propagated these specimens, often not knowing what conditions they needed or what the result would look like.

The earliest mention in Hertfordshire of seeds from India was at Cashiobury, near Watford, where Moses Cook (d. 1715), gardener to the second Earl of Essex, had little success with 'thirteen sorts of strange seeds ... from Goa'. He managed to raise ten of them but lost nine during the first year. The remaining specimen succumbed the following year 'for want of a green-house'.[83]

Much more success was had at Wormleybury. As Bisgrove states, 'few private gardens can have had such an important role in this sphere [plant introductions] as Wormleybury'.[84] Sir Abraham Hume II (1749–1838), Company director, inherited Wormleybury in 1772 and, with his wife Amelia and head gardener James Mean, set about cultivating exotics.[85] They cultivated many rare plants, including those from the East Indies and India, between 1785 and 1825 and numerous examples still survive today.

James Mean was the editor of the second edition of *Abercrombie's Practical Gardener* (1817) and of *The Gardener's Companion or Horticultural Calendar* (1820), and also wrote to and addressed the Horticultural Society of London. He received the silver medal for his paper 'On the Management of Orange, Lemon and Citron Trees, at Wormleybury, Herts', read to the Society on 7 January 1817, and was praised by Joseph Sabine in his article on the Stove at Wormleybury, read to the Society on 5 August 1817, who noted 'the peculiar success of Sir Abraham Hume's gardener, in the management of these exotics'.[86] This stove was designed for the raising of exotic plants and was kept at a temperature of 65–70°F.[87] Sabine stated that the plan was not particularly novel but was 'admirably suited to the purposes for which it was designed'. He gives the dimensions, 17 feet 9 inches by 12 feet 6 inches, and describes the complicated method of conducting hot air from the adjoining 'shed' around the edge of a tan pit (4 feet deep x 12 feet 6 inches x 5 feet 9 inches) which took up all the interior floor space, apart from a path around the edge. Plants were put on stands above the flue and creepers trained up on wires. There were glazed sloping lights all round to prevent plants becoming misshapen due to phototropism and one end of the building was removable to enable the transport of large plants.

The plants inside this and many other stoves and glass houses at Wormleybury were obtained from diverse sources. The Humes were well-known in horticultural circles both in England and abroad, and correspondence with Dr William Roxburgh, Superintendent of the Calcutta Botanic Garden, survives. One undated letter from Roxburgh, then in England, to an unknown correspondent, refers to his 'kind offer of a box of succulents' to take back to India with him. He asks him to send them to 'Lee, and Kennedy Nurserymen to be placed with a Box of growing plants, ordered by Lady Hume for the Botanic Garden at Calcutta'.[88]

Curtis' *Botanical Magazine* contains text and an illustration of a *Crinum amabile* from Hume's garden, entitled 'Sir Abraham Hume's Crinum'.[89] This flower was discovered flourishing in Wormleybury garden by Major Albert Pam, a twentieth-century owner of Wormleybury, in 1927.[90] It was also the subject of a letter to the Horticultural Society from the Reverend William Herbert, who raised a *Crinum augustum* from the Calcutta Catalogue, only for it to turn out to be 'the same plant as Sir Abraham Hume's Crinum named amabile in the *Botanical Magazine*, pl. 1605; and that it is now well known at Calcutta to be so'.[91]

According to Smith's *Exotic Botany*, Andrew's *Botanist's Repository* and the *Botanical Register*, many species were first cultivated at Wormleybury upon their introduction to England. Smith reported 'Dr Roxburgh … has sent Lady Hume a fine young tree of this species [*Dillenia speciosa*, Malabar] which is now in a very thriving state. It is presumed to be the first ever brought alive to Europe'.[92] He also sent *Stratiotes alismoides* to her, 'in whose stove it blossomed last autumn, not heard of in any other collection'.[93] The seed of *Rosa indica odoratissima* was sent to Hume and he introduced the white pomegranate (*Punica granatum* fl. Alba) in 1796, which flowered in 1799. A tree paeony, brought back by Captain J. Prendergast on the HMS *Hope*, bloomed at Wormleybury in 1806 and by 1826 was said to have reached a height of 7 feet and a circumference of 40 feet.[94] Captain Robert Welbank added the Maiden's Blush (*Camellia japonica*), and the large Mandarin orange (*Citrus nobilis*) arrived in 1805. In 1810 came one of the most important and influential imports, the first Tea Rose from China, Hume's Blush Tea Scented China Rose (*Rosa odorata*, or *Rosa indica fragrans*).[95]

Major Pam discovered 65 species that were growing at Wormleybury in Sir Abraham's time: 'most were stove or greenhouse plants of which 23 were shrubs, 12 climbers, 4 bulbous, 9 perennial herbs and 4 orchids. There were also 9 hardy perennial or biennial herbs, 1 hardy shrub and 1 hardy annual'.[96] Given the difficulties in transporting these plants from India before the advent of Wardian cases, and then persuading them to flourish, this is a remarkable achievement.

Some of the major players in the gaining and spending of Company fortunes in Hertfordshire thus set out some fine estates as a sign that they had arrived. Few stayed for long but the landscapes designed by Repton,

Bridgeman and others survived, albeit often altered, for many years. However, these new grandees were not the only ones to benefit from the East India Company. Many others, from the aristocracy to the lesser gentry, held shares in the Company and received dividends and other payments which could well have been spent on beautifying and developing their estates. One example was the Hale family at Kings Walden Bury, whose accounts in the 1650s include a receipt for £1,200 from India.[97] The Reverend John Olive, Rector of Ayot St Lawrence in the mid nineteenth century, not only had dividends from the Company but relatives still in the service.[98] He used the parish registers to doodle a plan of his orchard which he annotated with the names of many of the old varieties of apples together with notes as to their best use and storage qualities.[99]

Captains in the East India Fleet could rise in the Company. Richard Hall (1720–1786), son of Mr Hall of Hertford, was Captain in the *Worcester* between 1761 and 1770 and rose to become a director between 1773 and 1786.[100] Alexander Hume captained the *Fox*, owned by his relative Abraham Hume of Wormleybury. George Cuming (?–1787), brother-in-law of Abraham Hume, rose from being captain of the *Royal Duke* in 1747 (also owned by Hume) to becoming a director between 1764 and 1772. This was a hazardous occupation and as likely to lead to

Figure 4.11 View of Ayot church across the park. Designed by Nicholas Revett for Lionel Lyde in the 1770s. PHOTOGRAPH BY KATE HARWOOD, 2006

death as to fortune; much safer was the business of marine insurance. Clive of India considered that marine insurer Richard Gildart of Totteridge 'was one of the largest holders of East India Company stock, whose interest should be sought' and indeed he became a director in 1759.[101]

Another source of Company money was property management. Lionel Lyde of Ayot St Lawrence, a West Indies tobacco baron, made a little more money by leasing and subleasing premises in London from the Company. He had inherited his estate through his wife (and cousin) and spent his money by adding a little temple, some avenues and a new church to form an eyecatcher from his mansion. This church was one of architect Nicholas Revett's few Greek Revival buildings and was based on the Temple of Apollo at Delos (Figure 4.11).

Garden parties were an important part of the social round, and, indeed, one of the reasons for 'improving' one's estate was to show off one's impeccable taste. Lyde's garden parties were notable enough to be reported on at least two occasions. At the consecration of the new church in 1779 the report in the *Gentleman's Magazine* wrote of the twenty-strong uniformed band which led the way to the church and of the wine and cakes served in tents after the service. The day was rounded off with 'innocent games' in the fields and an 'elegant dinner' provided at the mansion.[102] A more fulsome report of a Harvest Home of 1783 was penned by the Rector, Mr Wheeldon,[103] describing the company, which

> consisted of Count de Guines, the French Ambassador; Earl & Countess of Salisbury; Countess of Clarendon; Lord Hyde; Lady Anne Cecil; Lady Charlotte Villiers; Lord and Lady Melbourne; Lord and Lady Grimston; Hon: Mr Stuart; Honbl Mr Lamb; Honbl: Mr York; Honbl Mr Nugent; Sir Ralph Milbank; Sir Charles, Lady and Miss Cocks; Sir Thomas and Lady Rumbold; Captain and Miss Rumbold; and many of the neighbouring Clergy and Gentry.

The festivities included the 'Militia Band of Musick' and elaborate arrangements for dancing: 'In the Entrance of a very venerable Grove fronting the House, a spacious covered Building was erected, floored and illuminated for Dancing.' The garden itself took centre stage:

> the whole Grove was beautifully enlightened and set off with Lamps of various colours and the Buildings were ornamented with Festoons of natural flowers. At proper distances from the four angles of the building, Tents were erected, two of which were served with Tea and other Refreshments; one was appointed for the

Militia Band, and the other for a Set of Country People, to sing Catches and Glees, and rural Songs in the Intervals between the Dances … In the inner Part of the Grove, another large rural Building was erected for the Village Feast, a Lamb roasted whole making the Center Dish. The old Tower, the Summer Houses, the several Buildings in the Gardens, and the Portico of the new Church, were very beautifully lighted up with Lamps of Different Colours … The Company then began to Dance in the covered Building and at Twelve o'Clock retired to an elegant supper. The House was illuminated with party-coloured Lamps hanging in Festoons. The Desert represented in a beautiful landscape of Houses, Farms, Barns, Stacks, etc and of Plowing, Sowing, Reaping, Mowing and all the Country Employments. The Ladies Dresses were extremely elegant, and adapted to the occasion with great Taste, their Heads being decorated with Wheat Ears and other Ornaments in Honour of the Evening. After Supper the Company danced in the Drawing-Room, and broke up at Four o'Clock, perfectly pleased with their Entertainment.

The nabobs of Hertfordshire did not flaunt their India connections with pagodas or Indian statues, domed palaces or minarets, but they were a closely linked community, working with (as with Benfield and Rumbold) or against (as with Sullivan and Rous) each other. The tentacles of the Company reached deep within polite society, affecting the standard of living of many of Hertfordshire's gentry. The nabobs were close enough to London to have London houses and the advantages of London society and taste but important enough in Hertfordshire for most of them to have served as sheriffs or deputy lieutenants. Many put their wealth towards embellishing their estates, employing Vanbrugh, Bridgeman, Repton, Mylne, Adam and Soane. Their gardens and landscapes reflect changing fashions, from late seventeenth- to early eighteenth-century geometric and formal, developing through wildernesses and serpentine lakes to the English landscapes of Brown and his followers, and finally to the gardenesque of Repton. A microcosm of the history of the eighteenth century, these landscapes detail the aspirations of their owners and the age, and are an important part of the history of Hertfordshire. They have suffered the ravages of time, becoming schools (Woodhall), golf courses (Broxbournebury and Moor Park), training centres (Ponsbourne) or nature reserves (Gubbins). The empire built half a world away has given Hertfordshire a legacy that is very precious and fragile. We should value it.

Notes

1. The 'long' eighteenth century was a phase of social and political history which started in the late seventeenth century and continued into the early nineteenth century. There were at least nine directors and many other Company men who acquired seats in Hertfordshire over this period.
2. *Nabob*: a European who made a fortune in the Orient, especially in India. From Portuguese *nababo,* from Hindi *nawab,* from the Arabic for governor, viceroy (Collins English Dictionary).
3. W. Foster, *Early travellers in India 1583–1615* (London, 1921).
4. This seems to have been a general seventeenth-century term for any temple.
5. P.J. Marshall, *East Indian fortunes. The British in Bengal in the 18th century* (Oxford, 1976), p. 214.
6. *Ibid.*
7. *Ibid.*, p. 159.
8. A. Farrington, *Trading places: The East India Company and Asia 1600–1834* (London, 2002).
9. Marshall, *East Indian fortunes*, p. 249.
10. *Ibid.*
11. J. Keay, *A history of India* (London, 2000), p. 373.
12. Marshall, *East Indian fortunes*, p. 217.
13. On various grounds including corruption and fraud while Governor General of India. However, Hastings was acquitted after a seven-year trial.
14. H. Repton, Wall Hall Red Book, from HALS, PC/163.
15. R. Williams, 'Vanbrugh's India and his Mausolea for England', in C. Ridgway and R. Williams (eds), *Sir John Vanbrugh and landscape architecture in baroque England 1690–1730* (Stroud, 2000). Fort St George had been acquired from the local Nawab in 1640, and developed into Madras. Bombay had come in 1661 as part of the Portuguese Catherine of Braganza's dowry when she married Charles II. For administrative convenience it was included in the manor of East Greenwich.
16. HALS, DE/AS/2172–2184, Abel-Smith estate papers.
17. J. Gibbs, *Book of Architecture* (London, 1728), Plate 53 shows garden front.
18. BLO, Gough Drawings a4. fo.64, *c.*1715–17.
19. D. Jacques, 'The Formal Garden', in C. Ridgway and R. Williams (eds), *Sir John Vanbrugh and landscape architecture in baroque England 1690–1730* (Stroud, 2000), p. 40.
20. Williams, 'Vanbrugh's India', p. 114.
21. The reports from seventeenth-century travellers in India are universally admiring of the 'fair' or 'noble' walls around the cities and along the coast.
22. Quoted by H. Colvin, *A Biographical dictionary of British architects 1600–1840*, 3rd edn (New Haven and London, 1995), p. 1008.
23. N. Salmon, *The history of Hertfordshire* (London, 1728), p. 225.
24. P. Kingsford, 'A history of Gobions in the parish of North Mymms, Hertfordshire', in P. Kingsford, R. Bisgrove and L. Jonas, *Gobions Estate North Mymms Hertfordshire* (Brookmans Park, 1993), p. 8.
25. *Ibid.*, p. 5.
26. Gloucestershire Record Office, D1245/FF25, map on vellum *c.*1735 showing plan of the Gobions estate, surveyed by Thos. Homes.
27. A. Jones (ed.), *Hertfordshire 1731–1800 as recorded in The Gentleman's Magazine* (Hatfield, 1993), p. 2.
28. G. Bickham (the Younger), *Beauties of Stow* (London, 1750).
29. *Ibid.*
30. *Gentleman's Magazine,* vol. 73, Pt.1, 1803, p. 88.
31. J.G. Park, 'The Directors of the East India Company 1754–1790', (PhD thesis, Edinburgh, 1977).

32. *The Ambulator or Stranger's Companion in a Tour around London*, 1774, pp. 72–73, quoted in Kingsford, 'A history of Gobions', p. 5.

33. W. Toldervy, *England and Wales described in a series of letters*, vol. 1 (1762), pp. 117–122.

34. H. Walpole, *History of the modern taste in gardening* (London, 1780).

35. Kingsford, 'A history of Gobions', p. 6.

36. Bodleian Library, Gough Drawings a4. fo.58.

37. Park, 'Directors of the East India Company'.

38. Jones, *Hertfordshire 1731–1800*, p. 249.

39. Anon., *The Michie family of Aberdeen* (privately printed, n.d.), quoted in Park, 'Directors of the East India Company'.

40. HALS, DE/Ga/35744–5 and 357447, Brookmans Park estate and Gaussen family papers.

41. HALS, DE/Ga/35751–2 and 35753, Brookmans Park estate and Gaussen family papers.

42. Guildhall, MS5881, File 2, Letter from John Michie to Jonathan Duncan 18 January 1786.

43. Willem G.J. Kuiters, 'Rumbold, Sir Thomas, first baronet (1736–1791)', *Oxford Dictionary of National Biography* (Oxford, 2004), www.oxforddnb.com/view/article/24270 (accessed 17/01/2007).

44. Park, 'Directors of the East India Company'.

45. W.G.J. Kuiters, 'William Paxton 1744–1824. Merchant and banker of Bengal and London', (PhD thesis, Leiden, 1992).

46. Connected with the zamindar and dealings with the Nawab of Arcot (*zamindar* were collectors of rent on land).

47. The National Archives, Kew, Public Acts 22, Geo III. (1782) HL/PO/PU/1/1782/22G3n89.

48. Park, 'Directors of the East India Company', p. 229.

49. HALS, DE/B1297/F1, Meetings with Thomas Leverton about Woodhall Park 1777–80.

50. Jones, *Hertfordshire 1731–1800*, p. 226.

51. BL, MSS Eur OEIC, note on Benfield as banker and creditor of Nawab of Arcot and notoriously corrupt.

52. BL, OIOC MSS Eur D788, letters of Sir Thomas Rumbold.

53. D. Moles, 'An able and skilful artist: the career of Paul Benfield of the English East India Company' (paper for Lincoln College, Oxford, 2000), quoting from a speech by Edmund Burke on the loans to the Nawab of the Carnatic given in the House of Commons in 1784.

54. P.J. Marshall, 'Benfield, Paul (1741–1810)', *Oxford Dictionary of National Biography* (Oxford, 2004), www.oxforddnb.com/view/article/2092 (accessed 17/01/2007).

55. HALS, DE/L/5414, estate records and Title Deeds from Messrs Longmore; see also HALS, DE/AS/1–4898.

56. BL, OIOC MSS Eur C307/1–C/307/5, IOR/H/128, IOR/H/130, IOR/H/104, IOR/H/277.

57. Park, 'Directors of the East India Company'.

58. Information about Broxbournebury derived from a number of archive sources including HALS, DE/Bb/E2 rental of Lord Monson's estate Broxbournebury, DE/Bb/E32 Memoranda Book of Jacob Bosanquet, DE/AS/4082, 4083, 4084, 4085 Title Deeds for Watkins Hall, DE/L/5005 Title Deeds for Hoddesdon; Linc Archives MON 16/1 Inventory of Broxbournebury for Lord Monson appraised to Jacob Bosanquet.

59. BL, OIOC IOR/L/MAR/A–B, India Office Maritime Records.

60. BL, IOR/E/3/97 f100v 17 Jan 1711 East India Company Letter Book 14, letter to Edward Harrison.

61. *Gentleman's Magazine*, vol. 2, 1732, p. 1083.

62. P. Sangster, *History of Balls Park, Hertford* (Hertford, n.d.).

63. HALS, A. Dury and J. Andrews, *A topographical map of Hartford-Shire* (1766; republished by the Hertfordshire Record Society in 2004).

64. K. Harwood, 'A Hertfordshire garden in the eighteenth century', *Herts Past and Present*, 3rd series, 2 (Autumn 2003), pp. 12–16.

65. RIBA Drawings Collection, BB88/1587, 1589, 1599, Wormleybury drawings.

66. BL, IOR/H/103 and BL, IOR/H/24.

67. Northamptonshire RO, SOX 352.

68. HALS, DE/Of/8/549, Oldfield collection.

69. J.E. Cussans, *History of Hertfordshire* III (London, 1881).

70. P. Dean, *Sir John Soane and the county estate* (Aldershot, 1999).

71. HALS, PC/163, photographs of Repton's Red Book for Wall Hall.

72. Department of the Environment List of Buildings of Special Architectural or Historic Interest, Borough of Hertsmere.

73. HALS, DP/3/29/9A, Wall Hall sale particulars, 1812.

74. I. Thomas, *Haileybury 1806–1987* (Hertford, 1987), p. 3.

75. Hertfordshire Gardens Trust and R. Bisgrove, *Hertfordshire gardens on Ermine Street* (Abbots Langley, 1996), p. 18.

76. R.G.C. Desmond, 'A Repton Garden at Haileybury', *Garden History Society Journal*, 6 (1978), pp. 16–19.

77. BL, OIR Records of EIC Haileybury MSS Eur D788.

78. C.M. Matthews, *Haileybury since Roman Times* (London, 1959), p. 163.

79. Park, 'Directors of the East India Company'.

80. HALS, DE/X2/14, 'Manor of Ponsbourne', *Cosmopolitan*, vol. III, No.7, May 1888.

81. HALS, DE/X2/7, MSS regarding the manor of Ponsbourne.

82. HALS, DE/X2/12, East Herts Archaeological Society visit report 22 June 1907.

83. D. Jacques and A.J. van der Horst, *The gardens of William and Mary* (London, 1988), p. 148.

84. Hertfordshire Gardens Trust and Bisgrove, *Hertfordshire gardens*, p. 20.

85. Amelia Egerton was the sister of the seventh and eighth Earls of Bridgwater of Ashridge. In the eighteenth century 'exotics' were any plants from overseas, not necessarily those needing a stove or cold frame.

86. Joseph Sabine was the brother of Mrs Henry Browne of North Mymms Park.

87. J.C. Smith, 'A record of a few special events. Matters relative to the Royal Botanic Garden at Kew', *Transactions of the Horticultural Society of London* (1838), Appendix 4.

88. Kew Inward Book, No.159.

89. Lindley Library, T. 1605, Curtis' *Botanical Magazine*, 39 (1814).

90. A. Pam, 'Wormleybury Gardens 1785–1825', *Journal of the Royal Horticultural Society*, 66 (1941), pp. 308–12.

91. *Transactions of the Horticultural Society of London*, 3 (1820).

92. J.E. Smith, *Exotic botany* (London, 1804), Tab. 2, 3.

93. *Ibid.*, Tab. 16.

94. J. Sabine, article about the stove at Wormleybury, *Transactions of the Horticultural Society of London*, 6 (1826), pp. 465–92.

95. Harwood, 'A Hertfordshire garden in the eighteenth century'.

96. Pam, 'Wormleybury Gardens'.

97. BL, Add. MSS 33,579 vol.VIII part 2, fo.269.

98. Rector 1830–1872: HALS, DE/X976, G. Hennessy, *Hertfordshire Incumbents – Alphabetical list*, 1918.

99. HALS, DP/10/1/3, Ayot St Lawrence parish register.

100. Park, 'Directors of the East India Company'; BL, IOR/L/MAR/A–B, maritime registers in the India Office Library.

101. Park, 'Directors of the East India Company'.

102. Jones, *Hertfordshire 1731–1800*, pp. 41–2.

103. HALS, DE/Cy/F8, Harvest Home Notes in the Chauncy Papers, 1783.

There are three known descriptions of the garden. Possibly the earliest one, written on two pages by Richard Dick, was found tucked in an old book in 1993.[2] This account must have been written between 1739 and 1765 as he visited the garden within a few days of seeing General Sabine's tomb at Tewin and the Great Bed of Ware at the Crown Inn. General Sabine was buried in 1739 and the Bed was moved to the Bull Inn in 1765. He would have approached the garden from Water Hall, called Watery Hall on the 1766 map. He wrote:

Third day the 18th: Went to Mr Brassee's at Rockford to see the Grotto, etc. 1st as you go in at the Gates you go up a Long Gravel Walk at the end whereof is a Leaden Statue on a pedestal representing Fame. Then you turn of your Left and then you go up a hill round and round till you come to the Top: of each Side as you go up there is Yew Hedges. Here and there is Seats cut in them. At the Top of the Hill is a fine Octagon Summer House, which commands a Prospect of the whole Garden and is richly Ornamented with fine Paintings. Then you come down the same way as you went up. And then you turn of your right and go into a Cave made of Flint which is under the Summer House, wherein is a Table upon which two Images stand one representing Death and the other Time. Their is two Windows shine into it or else it would be totally Dark. Then you come out and on your Right hand is an Aviary or place for Doves and on the left an Aviary for small singing and Canary Birds. Then before the Cave is a Large Oblong Fishpond where you see vast quantities of Fresh Water Fish and round the end of the Pond is Large peices of flint to represent small rocks and one peice is very much like a Busto. Then beyond this is an Octagon Bacon. On one Side is a piece of Shell Work where by Turning a cock a hundred Fountains and more play into the Water. In the middle of this Bason is Neptune standing with [h]is foot upon the Head of a Dolphin surrounded with Large Peices of Flint to represent rocks. Then you go [to] the Grotto where you go down a few Steps. On each side of you is Walls of Flint. Then he unlocks an iron Door where you go into the grotto. The bottom is paved with curious small pebbles from Black Heath, in a curious manner and on the great Wall afront the grotto is fine Shells, two small marble Basons of each side of the Door Way and one opposite. Then you go into the Grotto which is richly ornamented with Shells and coloured Flints, a Large Bason in the middle of it and fine marble Seats whereon you set. Then the Gardiner turns a Cock and fountains all round from the outside into the inside and one from the rock and several play over your head into the Bason. Then you go down a Few Steps into the Cold Bath paved with Marble and fine Stone and richly Ornamented with Painting. Then we came out and turn[e]d of our right and went [up] a little Hill over the Cold Bath where is a fine built Chimney round and like the fire a ... Bomb bursting out, the which chimney is for a fire in the Dressing Room. Then we came down and went by one Side of the Cold Bath the wall of Which is painted to represent a Door and two Windows. Then we came out, but besides their is Statues, Fountains etc ... '.[3]

There is also a mention of the garden in the diary of George William Harris, Rector of Egglescliffe, Durham. It was written in 1757 while he was staying at Panshanger, the home of the Dean of Durham, about 3 km north-west of Roxford. 'Mond[a]y july 4th. Tour w[i]th the D[ea]n in his Postchaise. Mr Bracey's, Roxford, a Banker in the city saw his Mount, w[hi]ch is some little distance fro[m] his house – made into a Garden – on the Top – a Grotto w[i]th water works, a great N[um]b[e]r of curious shells – all Gothic.'[4]

The last account is by Thomas Green, organist at All Saints, Hertford.[5] He visited the garden in 1775 and wrote about it and other houses and gardens nearby in a poem entitled 'Hertford and its Environs':

> See Roxford next a place retired
> but for its garden much admired
> These works of nature and of art
> Their various beauties do impart.
> A moat, a summer house, a cave
> An aviary too you have:
> Whose various birds you see and hear
> Whose melody delights the ear
> A bath that's elegant and neat
> And for the purpose quite compleat
> Adorn'd with paintings well designed
> By chosen artists of the kind
> But this the grotto far excels
> Which is enriched with choicest shells
> And ornaments of different kind
> To charm the eye and please the mind.
> And here a curious fountain plays
> Which throws the water different ways
> Above, below, on every side
> In plenteous streams both far and wide
> Where they disposed to lock you in
> They soon could wet you to the skin
> By curious art and man's device
> They'd do it for you in a trice;
> Indeed they never are so rude
> Unless a blockhead should intrude.

It is surprising that so far no clues have been found for the origin of this wonderful garden. There are, however, possible links with another grotto nearby at Ware, which has recently been restored. It too has a shell-encrusted entrance, an octagonal summerhouse and a room paved with small round stones. This grotto was built by a Quaker named John Scott, who finished the first part of it in 1764.[6]

The Brasseys, who owned Roxford throughout the eighteenth century, were London bankers and also Quakers. The two families must have known each other as they both would have attended the same Meeting House in Hertford. So, possibly, John Brassey or the first Nathaniel Brassey made the Roxford garden.

It is not known exactly when the Roxford garden was dismantled but it must have been between 1775 and 1789 because on Thomas Green's poem is a pencilled note which says, 'This place is now a mere wilderness. The moat, summerhouse and aviary, grotto, fountain and bath destroyed and the materials sold to Mr Alderman Kirby.' Mr Alderman Kirby died in 1789 and the grotto was in good order in 1775.[7] So it would seem that the second Nathaniel Brassey, who inherited Roxford in 1763, must have been responsible for its destruction. The fashion in gardens was changing and he may have been influenced by William Baker, who was shaping the landscape of Bayfordbury on the other side of the river by creating vistas with carefully planted trees.

It is recorded in *The Accounts of Thomas Green 1742–1790* that Green bought a stove, grate and fender at the sale of the widow of the first Nathaniel Brassey on 19 December 1786.[8] This sale was held three months after the death of Mrs Brassey and the stove may be the one mentioned by Richard Dick after his visit to the Roxford grotto. This *might* indicate that the garden was dismantled in 1786.

William Baker bought Roxford Manor in 1801 to add to his extensive estate of Bayfordbury. Bayfordbury Mansion was on the south of the river Lea and, as he already owned Hertingfordbury Park, the purchase of Roxford gave him an uninterrupted view of his own property along the north bank of the Lea, to plant and landscape as he pleased. The 1838 tithe map and award for Hertingfordbury shows the site of the Roxford garden as a coppiced wood named Grotto Wood.[9] It was recorded by that name in 1834 in the Bayfordbury Record Book: 'The vacant spaces in Grotto Wood left by fallen timber last year planted with Oak, Larch and Spruce Firs'.[10]

There is another interesting reference to Grotto Wood in the Record Book in 1859: 'Grotto underwood cut and the principal part of the Yews taken down with other Trees'. It is possible these yews formed the hedges described by Richard Dick, and some yews grow there to this day. At some time aconites, snowdrops and philadelphus were planted, probably by the Bakers during the nineteenth century. Grotto Wood as it was recorded by the Ordnance Survey in the 1870s is shown in Figure 5.2.

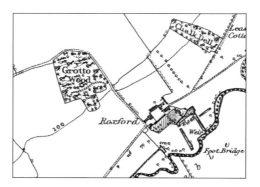

Figure 5.2 Detail of the Ordnance Survey first edition map sheet XXXVI, 6 inches to the mile, 1883, showing Roxford and Grotto Wood. REPRODUCED BY KIND PERMISSION OF HALS

Water Hall Farm, on which Grotto Wood is situated, had been let to tenants of the Bayfordbury estate from the beginning of the nineteenth century until it was sold in 1945 to the sitting tenants, A. Grubb & Son. The farm is described in the sale catalogue as 'an important mixed farm with valuable sand and gravel beds'.[11] The Grubbs extracted gravel and sand as well as running a mixed farm. In the 1970s Mr Grubb sold the farm to Mr Render, who subsequently sold it to Starmin (Star Quarrys). The present name of the company is SQ Environmental. Gravel pits were dug in the area around Grotto Wood at the end of the twentieth century and were then used as landfill sites.

The discovery of the eighteenth-century descriptions has aroused much interest in this forgotten garden since 1994. In March 1995 Christopher Currie was asked by the Hertfordshire Gardens Trust to carry out an archaeological survey of the garden earthworks in Grotto Wood. His research is recorded in *Hertfordshire Archaeology* vol.13 (1997–2003). He states, 'It [Grotto Wood] was surrounded by a large waste disposal tip and it was considered appropriate to record the garden remains in case they and its surroundings should be affected by the extension of the tip in the future.' Currie's plan of the earthworks is shown in Figure 5.3.

12. Varia Lane, niece of Meta and Stuart Hogg, who were tenants of Roxford from 1915 to the 1930s, recalled that Henry Baker organised an amateur excavation in Grotto Wood. He cut a trench into the mounds, uncovered the protected spring-head and discovered some wooden drainage conduits in the field below the wood. She thought that he was trying to find the chapel (which was built at Roxford soon after 1066). See Andrews, 'Roxford'.
13. HALS, DE/X629/P1, Bayfordbury estate map, 1807.
14. C.K. Currie and S. Wade, 'An assessment of a historic garden site at Grotto Wood, Roxford, Hertingfordbury, Hertfordshire' (unpublished report for Groundwork Hertfordshire and SQ Environmental, 2001).

Bibliography

Primary sources

Dick, R., two pages of a mid eighteenth-century journal in private ownership

Dury, A. and Andrews, J., *A topographical map of Hartford-Shire* (1766; republished by the Hertfordshire Record Society in 2004)

Hampshire Record Office, ref. 9M73/958, diary of the Reverend George William Harris, Rector of Egglescliffe, Durham, 1757

Hertfordshire Archives and Local Studies (hereafter HALS), DE/X269/B9, Bayfordbury estate sale particulars, 1945

HALS, DE/X629/P1, Bayfordbury estate map, 1807

HALS, DSA4/51/1 and 2, Tithe map and award for Hertingfordbury, 1838

HALS, PC/369, photocopies of the Bayfordbury Record Book, 1759–1906

Hertford Museum, book containing Thomas Green's poem 'Hertford and its Environs'

John Innis Institute, Bayfordbury Record Book 1759–1865 (photocopies at HALS, PC/369)

Secondary sources

Andrews, W.F., 'The manor of Roxford', *Transactions of the East Hertfordshire Archaeological Society*, 6 (1916–18)

Currie, C., 'An archaeological survey of garden earthworks in Grotto Wood, Roxford, Hertingfordbury', *Hertfordshire Archaeology*, 13 (1997–2003)

Currie, C.K. and Wade, S., 'An assessment of a historic garden site at Grotto Wood, Roxford, Hertingfordbury, Hertfordshire', (unpublished report for Groundwork Hertfordshire and SQ Environmental, 2001)

Perman, D., *A new guide to Scott's Grotto* (Ware, 1991)

Perman, D., *Scott of Amwell: Dr Johnson's Quaker critic* (Ware, 2001)

Sheldrick, G., *The accounts of Thomas Green 1742–1790* (Hertford, 1992)

CHAPTER SIX

The influences behind the creation of John Scott's grotto

Lottie Clarke

Scott's Grotto at Amwell End, Ware, is a series of eighteenth-century subterranean chambers.[1] It is Hertfordshire's most complete example of the grotto-builder's art, and almost the only surviving original feature of the garden created at Amwell House by John Scott in the 1760s. Scott's home still exists but it has been absorbed into the campus of Hertford Regional College and retains little of its eighteenth-century identity, and a nearby residential street named Scott's Road is the only clue to the earlier ownership of the land which is now, apart from the grotto and a summerhouse, covered in housing. 'Scott of Amwell' was a Quaker poet, businessman and philanthropist who achieved renown through his poetry and his shell-lined grotto.[2] After his death in 1783, his house and garden had several owners. During the latter half of the nineteenth century, the grotto was open to the public and advertised as a 'wonderful place' (Figure 6.1). Visitors were encouraged to travel by rail to the nearby station and take tea in the grounds. The garden in which the grotto was situated was sold off for housing and by the 1960s the grotto was neglected and vandalised. A full-scale restoration, spearheaded by the Ware Society, was completed in 1991, and the grotto is now designated a Grade I listed building. The porch and summerhouse were rebuilt and shells and minerals were sourced worldwide to restore the interior (Plate 6.1 and Figure 6.2).[3]

Scott's Grotto was one person's interpretation of a type of feature stretching back to antiquity. Although it is unlikely that Scott had only one source of inspiration for his project, it is possible to investigate the influences which may have contributed towards his decision to build a grotto, and to its design.

The creation of grottoes as garden features evolved from early humans' use of natural caves. Prehistoric cave paintings of wild animals

Figure 6.1 A Victorian handbill advertising Scott's grotto as a destination for day-trippers from London. 'Arma' is a corruption of *oreille-de-mer*, a Channel Island shell used extensively to decorate the chambers and alcoves. Palm Pillar Room, Hermit's Cave and Quaker's Room were names given to various chambers in the nineteenth century. REPRODUCED BY KIND PERMISSION OF HODDESDON LIBRARY, LOCAL STUDIES

Figure 6.2 The porch to the grotto is a modern re-creation dating from the early 1990s. Windows allow light to illuminate the underground chambers. A solid door has been added to make the building easier to secure. REPRODUCED BY KIND PERMISSION OF DAVID PERMAN

were perhaps created to enhance the hunters' chances of success and, consequently, these caves became associated with magical powers and mythology. In ancient Greece caverns which featured huge natural stalactites were sacred places consecrated to gods. Many had springs within them and this connection with life-giving water imbued them with spiritual significance. By the Renaissance, a period of fascination with all things classical, it became fashionable to create grottoes as spiritual or cultural statements. They fell into two categories: those which were rustic in style and looked like caves; and others which were architecturally sophisticated temple-like buildings – *nymphaea* (dedicated to nymphs) – which housed allegorical classical statues and fountains. Their cool shady depths were particularly welcome during hot Mediterranean summers. The cultural effect of the Renaissance spread northwards throughout Europe in the sixteenth and seventeenth centuries, and large numbers of spectacular grottoes were constructed in the most fashionable gardens of the period. They often included elaborate water features designed to impress or amuse guests and were used for entertaining, or as the backdrop for outdoor theatrical productions. It was only in the eighteenth century that the fashion for grottoes reached Britain, a result of landowners undertaking the Grand Tour, combined with growing political and financial security. Grottoes were visual links to the classical world, embodiments of the prevailing picturesque style in gardening, symbols of the forces of nature and, for those with creative leanings, a place in which to think and write. The grotto is a source of poetic inspiration and contemplation but also a startling and sudden contrast between the natural, outer world of the garden and the mysterious and contrived artificiality inside.

Scott may have drawn upon many sources of inspiration for his creation and design of a grotto. They can be categorised under three broad headings: literary, Quaker and local.

Literary influences

One of the major literary figures of the period, the poet Alexander Pope, is credited with stimulating an interest in the creation of grottoes in Britain during the eighteenth century. In 1720 work began on an elaborate subterranean passage between two parts of his garden at Twickenham, as well as on a grotto. He conceived his creation as a '*Musaeum*' or '*Nymphaeum*', a place where muses might communicate

and John Lettsom, who had a botanical garden in Camberwell, the subject of a poem by Scott. Cockfield was an avid collector of seeds and plants from overseas, many of which he gave to Scott.

As Quakers were frequently involved in industrial activities such as copper or iron production, they experimented in the decorative use of industrial by-products such as slag and clinker. William Champion, for example, first developed the commercial production of zinc at Warmley House near Bristol. His extensive grotto complex was almost entirely composed of clinker, and its cascades and pools were fed by water from a man-made thirteen-acre lake, excavated to act as a reservoir for the watermills on the estate.[12] Many Quakers also developed passions for collecting geological specimens, as well as plants. One such, Thomas Goldney, a merchant from Bristol, benefited from his connections within the close-knit Quaker banking and shipping community, who funded privateering voyages and thereby enabled him to import shells in large quantities. He also employed local people to collect West Country fossils and minerals for his grotto, begun in 1737. Statues, cascades and fountains (operated by a pumping system) decorated the large structure, which was both above and underground. It took twenty-seven years to complete and, as with Scott and Pope, Thomas Goldney was overtaken by the passion for collecting shells, fossils and minerals.[13] It is certain that he did not employ a professional designer for his garden and seems, like Scott, to have been responsible for the design of both the garden and grotto himself. Although both men were known to have been involved in the decoration of their grottoes, the enormous volume of material which had to be affixed to the interior walls would certainly have necessitated the use of paid labour. Goldney, for example, employed John Warwell to undertake the decorative shellwork around the pool.[14] Scott is known to have visited Bristol and, as Goldney welcomed visitors to his garden and invited fellow Quakers to social events in his home, it is possible that the poet may have seen this fantastic grotto, and also perhaps the one at Warmley, and been inspired to create one for himself.

Local influences

In Hertfordshire another Quaker grotto, which Scott possibly knew well, was at Roxford, the home of the Brassey family, five miles from Amwell. It had probably been created some time in the first half of the eighteenth century and was an elaborate affair, incorporating shellwork

and water features. A description by Richard Dick of the grotto at
Roxford describes a floor laid with 'curious small pebbles from Black
Heath'.[15] Patterns of coloured pebbles were also set into the floor of
Scott's grotto (Figure 6.5). They were uncovered during the extensive
restoration of the building in the 1990s.[16] Dick goes on to describe the
walls at Roxford as being 'richly ornamented with Shells and coloured
Flints', as were those in the grotto at Amwell. There was one significant
difference between the two neighbouring grottoes: according to Dick, at
Roxford 'the Gardiner turns a Cock and fountains … play over your head
into the Bason'. It is not clear from the description whether this feature
was designed as a highlight of the journey through the garden and was
turned on in order to impress guests with the hydraulic system needed to

Figure 6.5 The original grotto floor is composed of a circular pattern of polished pebbles, as in
Scott's own poem 'where glossy pebbles pave the varied floors'. REPRODUCED BY KIND PERMISSION OF
DAVID PERMAN

send water shooting into the air; or whether it was a form of *giochi d'acqua*, or water game, the gardener secretly unleashing the water from the fountain to trap and possibly amuse the unwary grotto visitor. Such conceits were popular in sixteenth- and seventeenth-century Italian gardens, but in eighteenth-century English gardens the prevailing taste was for water presented in a naturalistic way. Scott did not incorporate any waterworks into his grotto, perhaps on the grounds of cost, perhaps because he was aware that they were no longer considered fashionable. William Shenstone wrote, on this subject, 'the fall of water is Nature's province – only the vulgar citizen … squirts up his rivulets in jettaux'.[17] The grotto at Roxford and the surrounding garden were demolished some time between 1775 and 1789 and the materials sold to an Alderman Kirby of Hertford.[18] No record exists to explain their eventual use. But, apart from the waterworks, as discussed above, Roxford bears many similarities to the grotto built by Scott.

In the 1720s, perhaps at the same time as the Brasseys were working at Roxford, Mary Caesar was creating a grotto at Benington Place, a few miles north of Amwell. Mary, a keen gardener, counted Jonathan Swift and Alexander Pope among her friends.[19] While no evidence has been discovered to prove Pope's involvement in the design of the grotto at Benington, it is very likely that he would have contributed suggestions as she developed her own ideas. Whether or not Scott ever saw this grotto is not recorded, but he may well have heard of it.

In 1764 Scott wrote, 'I have finish'd my Shell Temple both the Inner room or Grotto and ye Portico, and now begun another cavern or Subterraneous Grot in ye side of the hill behind the former'.[20] This indicates that he felt his grotto was complete, but he was nevertheless embarking on further excavations into the hillside. No written explanation exists of Scott's decision to extend, although one possible clue appears in a letter: 'indeed my dear friend to a benevolent Mind I scarce know a more pleasing Amusement than employing the Industrious Labourer: what greater satisfaction to the Eye than to behold them chearfull under unceasing Toil, or to the Contemplative Mind than to imagine their Indigent families enjoing the scanty produce of their labour'.[21] Similarly, Scott employed teams of up to fifty local men to repair the turnpike between Ware and Hertford, which ran past the front of Amwell House and was the route by which the Scott family travelled to meetings at the Friends' Meeting House in Hertford; it was

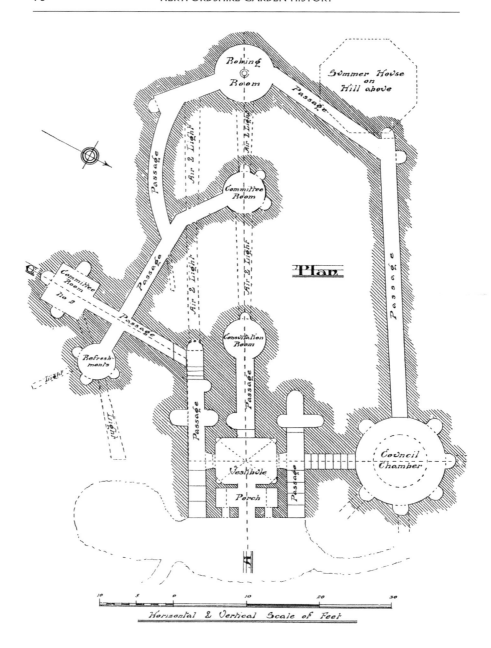

Figure 6.6 Nineteenth-century plans showing the extent of the subterranean network and points where light and air are introduced into the chambers and passages. The position of the summerhouse is at the highest point in the garden, directly above the grotto. The chamber names were nineteenth-century additions. REPRODUCED BY KIND PERMISSION OF THE EAST HERTS ARCHAEOLOGICAL SOCIETY FROM THE ARTICLE BY R.T. ANDREWS, 1899

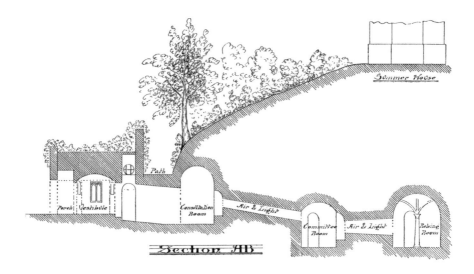

in very poor condition in comparison to others nearby. His grotto may have been extended as a further philanthropic gesture to provide continuing employment for the labourers, and the work possibly served as a means of obtaining hardcore for road improvements. In either case, using the by-product of his excavations to improve the road would have satisfied his Quaker wish not to despoil the countryside as a result of his grotto-building. Another explanation for Scott's expansion of the grotto might be the series of smallpox outbreaks in the eighteenth century. So fearful was he of contracting the disease that, in 1766, he took the risky decision to be inoculated, and between 1740 and 1760 he rarely ventured into London, instead preferring to invite his friends to visit him in Hertfordshire. He perhaps wanted to develop and embellish the grotto still further as an extra inducement to lure them from the capital. The final dimensions dwarf those of any contemporary grotto (Figure 6.6). Windows of coloured glass and air vents introduced morning sunlight into the chambers to illuminate the decorated interior. The network of passages which links the ventilated chambers maintains a cool dry atmosphere, pleasant at any time of year.

A visitors' book, begun in 1779 and continuing until 1787, four years after Scott's death, contains over 3,000 names. It shows not only that the Quaker poet was as keen as any socialite to show off his property, but also that the grotto attracted interest from people in all walks of life, from England, Europe and America. Dr Johnson, tradesmen, local schoolchildren and members of the aristocracy all added their names and comments to the book after they had been shown the grotto and garden by Scott's gardener.

The raw materials for the grotto

Scott's shellwork is far removed from the elaborate style in the grotto at Goodwood (Figure 6.7). The Duchess of Richmond and her daughters designed the building there as a sophisticated garden room for entertaining. At Amwell, Scott created the naive effect himself. He probably found the inspiration for the design of his grotto from a variety of sources, poetic and real, but obtaining the materials was an altogether greater and more practical challenge. He did not use tufa or artificial stalactites to emulate nature, as at Painshill (Figure 6.8), nor statuary and waterworks as at Goldney and Roxford, perhaps due to financial constraints. Instead he created in the style favoured by Pope – a combination of natural objects, coloured glass and skylights to create what his friend Dr Johnson described as a 'fairy hall'.[22] It would have been time-consuming to amass the considerable amount of natural material needed to decorate the interior. Quantities of cockle shells, fossils and white quartz were requested from John Turner, a minister in Devon 'for the completion of this work, in which he frequently exerted his own manual labour'.[23] They can still be seen on the walls of the room named the 'Council Chamber' in the nineteenth century, together with large red pebbles and slabs of mica schist similar to those found at Lympstone – Turner's parish.[24] John Hoole, a friend, first brought Dr Johnson to see the grotto. Hoole was an auditor with the East India Company, which may have given him unparalleled access to supplies of foreign shells, often used as ballast in ships returning to Britain from the West Indies and America. Scott's friend Joseph Cockfield was commissioned to purchase many of the Caribbean, South Pacific and Channel Island shells used to line the walls, and 'melted glass', 'lustres or isicles',[25] to frame the windows and reflect light into the chambers below, as in Pope's grotto in Twickenham. Cockfield's father, Zachariah, was a wealthy timber merchant with trading links in the Baltic and a shareholding in South Sea Annuities, so undoubtedly his business contacts would have been exploited in the search for decorative materials. Joseph Cockfield was himself a friend of Captain James Cook,

Figure 6.7 The grotto built at Goodwood House, Sussex, between 1739 and 1746 was used for entertaining. A fantasy of elaborate shellwork was bathed in light reflected from mirrors hung on the walls. The design is reminiscent of the sophisticated interiors of grand houses, and Scott's creation is crudely executed in comparison. PHOTOGRAPH BY ANNE ROWE, 2000, REPRODUCED BY KIND PERMISSION OF THE GOODWOOD ESTATE COMPANY

Figure 6.8 The grotto at Painshill Park, Surrey, was built to imitate a cave. Elaborate frameworks were constructed to accommodate tufa, minerals and felspar in a naturalistic style.
PHOTOGRAPH BY ANNE ROWE, 2000

who he almost certainly would have asked to bring back specimens from his long voyages. The precedent for grotto owners to prevail upon their friends and acquaintances for the supply of materials to decorate the interiors was set by Pope, Goldney, Shenstone and members of the aristocracy. Contacts of Mary Caesar in turn asked their own acquaintances to provide her with shells from places including Guernsey and the Isle of Wight.[26] Scott, however, did not overlook an interesting local geological phenomenon: he incorporated several examples of Hertfordshire Puddingstone into his decorations.

The inspirations for John Scott's grotto were undoubtedly many and varied, originating in the literary, Quaker and Hertfordshire circles he frequented. His own poetic leanings would have prompted him to create a place to stimulate his imagination as he describes in his poem Epistle I, 'The Garden':[27]

> Where, 'midst thick oaks, the subterraneous way
> To the arch'd grot admits a feeble ray;
> Where glossy pebbles pave the varied floors,
> And rough flint-walls are deck'd with shells and ores,
> And silvery pearls, spread o'er the roofs on high,
> Glimmer like faint stars in a twilight sky;
> From noon's fierce glare, perhaps, he pleas'd retires,
> Indulging musings which the place inspires.

This personal ambition would have been reinforced by his admiration of fellow poets Pope and Shenstone, who had already created their own grottoes. In literary circles, he would have wished to be seen as having a fashionable garden worthy of visiting. As he did not include idolatrous statues in the grotto, the majority of it was underground, and he did much of the work himself, he could not be accused of indulging in ostentatious or extravagant behaviour unsuitable for a Quaker.

Scott's Grotto is one man's eclectic creation, inspired by a variety of sources – poetic, horticultural and social. These came together in a unique monument to a complex personality – keen gardener, successful poet, political commentator, philanthropist and Quaker. It is an outstanding example of the eighteenth-century love of amateur garden design indulged in by the wealthy and well-connected.

Scott's Grotto is situated in Scott's Road, Ware, and is regularly open to the public, and to parties by appointment. Further details are available on www.scottsgrotto.org.uk

Notes

1. The southernmost part of the town of Ware, where John Scott lived, lay south of the river Lea in the parish of Great Amwell, hence the name of the locality, Amwell End, and the name by which the poet is commonly known, 'Scott of Amwell'.

2. An authoritative biography of John Scott has been written by local historian, David Perman, which has proved an invaluable source for the present essay: D. Perman, *Scott of Amwell: Dr Johnson's Quaker critic* (Ware, 2001).

3. The project to restore the grotto was managed by David Perman, who was secretary of the Ware Society between 1978 and 1992.

4. A. Beckles Willson, *Alexander Pope's grotto* (London, 1998).

5. A. Pope, *Epistle to Lord Burlington* (London, 1731).

6. www.soton.ac.uk/~sdb2/unconnected.htm, S. Bending and A. McRae (eds), 'William Shenstone, 'Unconnected Thoughts on Gardening' (1764)', p. 2.

7. D. Perman, *Scott of Amwell: Dr Johnson's Quaker critic* (Ware, 2001), p. 56, quoting Dr Johnson. See G.B. Hill (ed.), *Lives of the English Poets, Samuel Johnson* (Oxford, 1905), III, p. 350.

8. Perman, *Scott of Amwell*, p. 73, quoting J. Scott, *Poetical works* (London, 1782; reprinted Farnborough, 1969), p. 260, Epistle 1. 'The Garden'.

9. Perman, *Scott of Amwell*, p. 72.

10. T. Tranter, *The Shell Grotto at Hampton Court House* (handout produced by the London Borough of Richmond on Thames for London Open House, 2000).

11. A collection of Scott's letters to Cockfield is held at the Friends House Library, Dimsdale MSS, and has been examined by David Perman in *Scott of Amwell*.

12. Advice Note 30 Warmley Conservation Area, published by South Gloucestershire Council, www.southglos.gov.uk

13. P. Stembridge, *Thomas Goldney's garden* (Bristol, 1996).

14. *Ibid.*, p. 8.

15. P. Bagenal, 'Roxford's forgotten grotto', *Follies*, 21 (1994), p. 3 and this volume, Chapter 5, quoting R. Dick, unpublished manuscript in private hands, undated.

16. D. Perman, *A new guide to Scott's Grotto* (Ware, 1991), p. 10.

17. www.soton.ac.uk/~sdb2/unconnected.htm, p. 5.

18. Bagenal, 'Roxford's forgotten grotto', p. 4.

19. A. Rowe, *Garden making and the Freman family: a memoir of Hamels* (Hertford, 2001), p. 49.

20. Perman, *Scott of Amwell*, p. 68, quoting Friends House Library, Dimsdale MSS, Folder 11/11, letter to Joseph Cockfield, 2 September 1764.

21. *Ibid.*, p. 64, quoting letter from Scott to Joseph Cockfield.

22. *Ibid.*, pp. 17, 152, quoting Hoole.

23. *Ibid.*, p. 73, quoting Hoole.

24. *Ibid.*

25. *Ibid.*, p. 68, quoting Friends House Library, Dimsdale MSS, Folder 11/11, letter to Joseph Cockfield, 2 September 1764.

26. Rowe, *Memoir of Hamels*, pp. 51–2, quoting letters to Mary Caesar in the 1720s preserved in the Caesar Papers at Rousham.

27. Perman, *Scott of Amwell*, p. 72, quoting Scott, *Poetical works*, p. 260, Epistle 1, 'The Garden'.

Bibliography

Secondary sources

Andrews, R.T., 'Scott's Grotto', *Transactions of the East Herts Archaeology Society* (1899)

Bagenal, P., 'Roxford's forgotten grotto', *Follies*, 21 (1994)

Beckles Willson, A., *Alexander Pope's grotto* (London, 1998)

Bennett, S., *Five centuries of women and gardens* (London, 2000)

Fearnley-Whittingstall, J., *The garden: an English love affair* (London, 2002)

Hill, G.B. (ed.), *Lives of the English Poets, Samuel Johnson* (Oxford, 1905)

Hobhouse, P., *The story of gardening* (London, 2002)

Hoole, J., *Life of John Scott* (London, 1785)

Jackson, H., *Shell houses and grottoes* (Princes Risborough, 2001)

Jellicoe, G. and S., *The Oxford companion to gardens* (London, 1986)

Jones, B., *Follies and grottoes* (London, 1989)

Perman, D., *A new guide to Scott's Grotto* (Ware, 1991)

Perman, D., *Scott of Amwell: Dr Johnson's Quaker critic* (Ware, 2001)

Pope, A., *Epistle to Lord Burlington* (London, 1731)

Rowe, A., *Garden making and the Freman family: a memoir of Hamels* (Hertford, 2001)

Scott, J., *Poetical works* (London, 1782; reprinted Farnborough, 1969)

Stembridge, P., *Thomas Goldney's garden* (Bristol, 1996)

Tranter, R., *The Shell Grotto at Hampton Court House* (handout produced by the London Borough of Richmond on Thames for London Open House, 2000)

Websites

www.captaincooksociety.com (accessed 8/12/2006)

www.soton.ac.uk/~sdb2/unconnected.htm (accessed 8/12/2006) Bending, S. and McRae, A. (eds), 'William Shenstone, 'Unconnected Thoughts on Gardening' (1764)'

www.southglos.gov.uk (accessed 8/12/2006)

CHAPTER SEVEN

Richard Woods
in Hertfordshire

Esther Gatland

> Brocket today is a fine realization of one of the best conceived
> and most fully executed schemes of the landscape school
> 'improving' on nature over a large area. Mr. Woods of Essex,
> within the rather narrow limits of the landscape school of his day,
> had a fine feeling for the picturesque.
>
> Avery Tipping, 1925[1]

The above comment is interesting for several reasons: it credits and
applauds Woods (unusual at that period), it reflects the view of the
landscape school still current at that time and for several decades after,
and it employs the word picturesque to describe Woods' philosophy.
Woods is only known to have worked at two sites in Hertfordshire
(despite considerable commissions in the surrounding counties), but
both of these, Newsells Park and Brocket Hall, are of some importance.

Richard Woods is something of an enigmatic figure. He was one of a
small group of mid eighteenth-century landscape improvers whose
reputations were largely eclipsed in the 150 years or so following their
deaths by that of Capability Brown. Recognition of Woods' talents, in
particular, hardly survived into the nineteenth century. There followed
the Victorian reaction against the landscaping of the previous century, an
attitude which persisted until a new appreciation of the style emerged in
the late 1950s and early 1960s, exemplified in Dorothy Stroud's
biography of Brown.[2] Woods' contribution to the English landscape is
now recognised and is being thoroughly researched. Following the initial
impetus from Nancy Edwards and Hugh Prince, and David Jacques'
account of Woods in *Georgian gardens*, Fiona Cowell has been working
for the last twenty-five years on the parks and gardens that Woods
designed throughout England.[3]

Plate 1.1 View of the hedge-lined *allées* of the early eighteenth-century woodland garden at St Paul's Walden Bury, from the north front of the house. PHOTOGRAPH BY ANNE ROWE, 2000

Plate 1.2 The Golden Valley, Ashridge Park: one of the finest surviving examples of the work of Capability Brown in Hertfordshire. PHOTOGRAPH BY G. CANNON, 1995

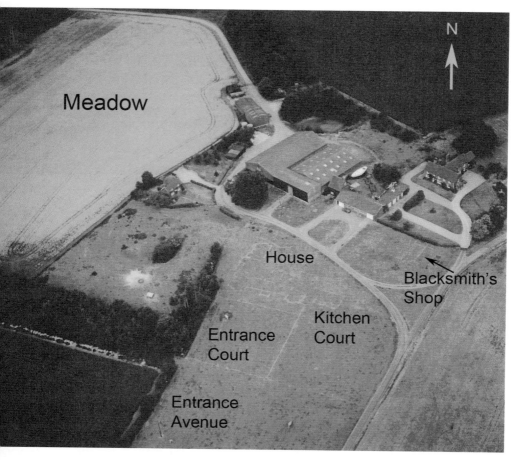

N

Meadow

House

Blacksmith's
Shop

Kitchen
Court

Entrance
Court

Entrance
Avenue

Plate 2.1 Aerial photograph of Quickswood from the south-west, *c.*2003.
PRIVATE COLLECTION © C. WILSON

Plate 10.1 The lodge in Clarence Park today with colourful bedding.
PHOTOGRAPH BY HAROLD SMITH, 2006

Plate 10.2 The replacement bandstand and new playground equipment, Clarence Park.
PHOTOGRAPH BY HAROLD SMITH, 2006

Plate 11.1 The outside of the north wall and end pier, showing part of the east hedge, Queenswood School. PHOTOGRAPH BY SALLY WRIGHT, 2006

Plate 11.2 Looking south through the pear pergola, Queenswood School.
PHOTOGRAPH BY SALLY WRIGHT, 2006

remnants of earlier, more formal planting as some are still in the form of squares, rectangles and lines, although it is not easy to see how the disparate blocks shown could have formed a coherent, formal whole. Square blocks of uniform planting projecting into the parkland from the shelterbelt appear to have been left, as have lines of trees marking the lines of two roads shown running through the park on the Dury and Andrews map. This would have been in accordance with Woods' normal practice of retaining much of the existing treescape and modifying it, rather than totally reworking it. He is seen doing the same thing at Brocket, ten years later.

On the 1788 estate map a path, which would have provided a leisurely promenade, runs some of the way around the park within the shelterbelt, crossing the entrance drive from the south and curving halfway up the east side of the park. In the middle of a clearing scooped

Figure 7.1 Detail of Dury and Andrews' county map of 1766, showing the park at Newsells Bury. REPRODUCED BY KIND PERMISSION OF HERTFORDSHIRE RECORD SOCIETY

Figure 7.2 View of the obelisk in Newsells Park. REPRODUCED BY KIND PERMISSION OF HALS [PICTURE COLLECTION]

Figure 7.3 Sketch of the hermitage in Newsells Park, *c.*1840. REPRODUCED BY KIND PERMISSION OF HALS (BARK/49A)

Brocket

In 1764 Woods' reputation was further enhanced when he was retained to create designs for Lord Arundel at Wardour – the commission running until 1771. Probably this prestige helped to gain him the opportunity to redesign the grounds at Brocket. Brocket Hall is first recorded as the seat of Sir John Brocket in the early sixteenth century. It then passed to the Reades and eventually to Thomas Winnington, by marriage, in 1711. Winnington was a politician with a distinguished career and a member of the Holland Park Group,[30] of which other members were the Reverend Desaguliers, Stephen Fox, Henry Fox, the Duke of Marlborough and Lord Hervey. Winnington would have been familiar with the latest fashions in garden design.

He commissioned plans for the improvement of Brocket Park c.1730 which have been attributed to Bridgeman,[31] but he apparently implemented only some of the suggestions – the blocks of woodland shown on the plan to the east and south sides of the park and some framing a vista to the Lemsford Mill entrance. A walled enclosure, probably a kitchen garden, had been constructed to the north-east of the house. Winnington had retained what seems to be a pretty enclosure to the south-west, with winding paths, an arbour and two square buildings on the corners nearest the river Lea: perhaps banqueting houses. The fields to the west had been decorated with circular copses and given a more manicured appearance, resembling Bridgeman's scheme for Richmond, Surrey, for George II.[32] Winnington's selective choices from Bridgeman's plans reflect the fact that in the 1730s opinion on design was still very divided. Aspects of the landscaping style and formality coexisted in some gardens until much later, as, for example, at Wrest Park, Bedfordshire, where Brown was only permitted to create informality around the edges of the formal Great Garden. The second Bridgeman plan of Brocket shows the river widened into a lake with a bridge giving access from the park to the gardens. A shelterbelt was established inside the brick wall bounding the park to the east.

Sir Matthew Lamb purchased Brocket Park in 1746 from the Winnington heirs, and in c.1752 commissioned a map (Plate 7.3) showing the park in order to record the house and park prior to his improvements.[33] He was a lawyer who had made an advantageous marriage to Charlotte, daughter of Thomas Coke of Melbourne, Secretary of State to Charles I. When Charlotte's brother died, Coke family money became available for grand designs at Brocket. Piecemeal reconstruction, following the footprint of the Elizabethan house, began *c*.1760 under the direction of architect James Paine.[34] The painting by Tomkins of 1768 (Plate 7.4),[35] hanging in the hall at Brocket, shows the completed house and the remodelled stables, but the river course resembles that shown on the 1752 map. A white, chinoiserie bridge crosses the river below the curlicue. The field boundaries to the west of the river are not apparent so had probably been removed already and possibly replaced by the two formal triangular blocks of trees planted to frame the view and lead the eye away. This could all have been the contribution of Matthew Lamb although Woods did use a similar device for the same purpose at Wormsley, Buckinghamshire.[36] It would appear that the North Lodges were already built by this time. Picturesque sketches of grazing cattle, sheep and horses add to the pastoral landscape. Tomkins was known as a precise depicter of the scene as it was, so it can reliably be assumed that this is what Woods saw when he arrived in 1770, two years after Sir Matthew's death.

The Lambs were an influential and wealthy family. Peniston (Matthew Lamb's son), the first Viscount Melbourne, had also married well; Elizabeth Milbanke brought money and prestige. She was close to the Prince Regent and related to the Spencers,[37] so they would presumably have had a free choice of improvers, yet chose Richard Woods in preference to Capability Brown.

According to Angus (in *Seats of the Nobility*, 1787), 'The Water and Out-grounds were laid out and disposed by Mr. Woods of Essex in the most luxuriant and masterly manner'. The *Copper Plate Magazine* repeats the attribution and pronounces the park, 'one of the most elegantly picturesque in the kingdom'.[38] It may have been Woods' expertise in the more intimate areas closer to the house, together with his use of scent and colour in his varied planting, which made him their choice. He had also worked with James Paine, the architect of the new hall, before: Paine and Woods had both worked for Lord Arundel at Wardour, also at Cusworth Hall, Yorkshire. Later they were together at Hare Hall in Essex (where employment of Woods is again recorded by Angus in 1791)[39] and possibly at Hardwick Park, County Durham.

Woods made an initial visit to Brocket in 1770, recorded in his letter to Lord Arundel,[40] and was apparently employed here until 1774. The estate accounts show a bill for six weeks' board for 'Mr. Woods and his clerk' in 1773 and he paid three visits in 1774, totalling seventeen days.[41] The estate papers also detail payments for building the stone bridge to Paine's design in 1774. Prior to this there were obviously long preparations – clearing the site and bringing the stone. The accounts give some interesting insights into the progress of the work. New work, sometimes involving considerable outlay, tended to be itemised separately. For example, between January and December 1774, £202 2s 9d was spent on 'carrying stones for bridge', and work by glaziers and plumbers in the hothouse and pinery cost £25 12s.[42] Between January and April 1775 'scythes, rakes and hoes for shrubbery' were purchased at a cost of £3 18s 11d. Accounts for 1773 and 1774 show as many as seventeen extra hands employed on work for Paine and Woods, so this was obviously when much of the landscaping and building was carried out. A carrier was paid £1 1s in June 1774 'for bringing orange trees from Northants', mushroom frames were thatched in October, and 'Pots for the hothouse' were bought in April of that year. There is no evidence in the estate accounts of any expense on new work in the gardens after Paine and Woods had left, so the beautiful plan by Thomas Pallett of 1798 is probably an excellent record of their achievements (Plate 7.5).[43]

Examination of this plan suggests that Woods made few alterations to the landscape in the park, probably just consolidating the earlier plantings. However, new groves were established in the eastern area, where the planting looks more varied – specimen trees interspersed with smaller trees and shrubs, looking more like Woods' mixed shrubbery

Figure 7.6 South Lodges and Screen at Brocket Park, in 2006. PHOTOGRAPH BY ESTHER GATLAND, 2006

than uniform tree blocks. There are wide, winding rides and interlinked grassy glades and cabinets with the appearance of an area to saunter in. The planting to the north-east has been strengthened, again with a variety of trees and, in two of the three versions of the Pallett map, a uniform avenue of trees runs roughly west through a wide, grassy expanse between the blocks of woodland.

Paine designed the South Lodges and Screen (Figure 7.6) which bear a distinct style reference to those at the north gate. Earlier drives from the south had entered the grounds by Lemsford Mill and followed the east bank of the river, curving around to a north entrance to the old Elizabethan house opposite the stables. After Paine's reconstruction of the house, the drive led to a new entrance on the south-east front.

Woods carried out the changes seen in the Broadwater at Brocket, eliminating the curlicue, carrying the embankment further downstream and building the cascade, thus creating the setting for Paine's new bridge. He was probably also responsible for the new approach to the hall, coming from the Lemsford Road, along the west side of the river, to cross the new bridge and sweep up to the south-east entrance to the mansion. This has undoubtedly created one of the most effective pieces of landscaping in the county (Figures 7.7 and 7.8). Avery Tipping comments, of the bridge,

> Its architectural excellence is enhanced by situation. As we approach it on the high ground on the west bank of the River Lea, we see it with its ends half shaded by trees, and through its arches the whole of the river pouring over the dam. We cross it to reach the east bank, when we rise up to the house level, and there get a full expanse of a lake bosomed in woods or well-timbered glades. The rising banks on each side were arranged with beech and other plantations to add height to the 'risings' and to give the impression of little valleys to the 'falls'.[44]

Most of the ancillary and garden buildings which add to the grandeur of the site were designed by James Paine. These include the Laundry complex to the north-east of the house, the Brewhouse, and the Dairy. However, the Fishing Arbour and Flint Bridge, along with various other structures shown in red in the park and pleasure grounds on Pallett's map of 1798, were probably by Woods.

Paine's new design for the house had given greater emphasis to the south-western front and the grandest rooms overlooked the river.[45] Woods' pleasure grounds were focused on this area, consisting of two

Figure 7.7 Brocket Park, by E.F. Burney, 1786. REPRODUCED BY KIND PERMISSION OF HALS
(DE/X55/Z2/13–14)

Figure 7.8 Brocket Hall in the first part of the nineteenth century, by J.C. Carter.
REPRODUCED BY KIND PERMISSION OF HALS (HAT/30)

walled gardens and extensive plantings along the riverbanks. Here he designed some undulating grassy areas between the house and the stables with small groups of forest trees on either side of the Broadwater to the west and south of the house. He may have augmented the swells of the banks by some earth movement as well as emphasising them by the placement of his groves of trees.

Along the riverside north-west of the house (Figure 7.9) he produced a landscaped area of single specimen forest trees interspersed with small clumps, viewed from a path on its east side which led northwards to a very different design. The 1798 plan shows this path dividing to run up either side of a long tongue of grass in which are very well-defined circular areas of planting where the plants appear much smaller – five specimen trees are dotted among these beds. It would appear that this planting is of shrubs, possibly small, choice trees – even some of the roses of which Woods was apparently so fond and included in many of his other designs around this time. He also often used honeysuckles (climbing up evergreens), jessamines, pyracanthas, 'strip'd alaternas, strip'd and plain ivy' and 'common and sweet flowers'.[46] It is possible that there were some herbaceous perennials in the front of the shrubs or even in beds on their own, such as Parnell described at Wooburn: 'you pass through fine old forest trees scattered irregularly, and amidst them some plots of flowers'.[47]

No planting plans survive for Brocket, nor Woods' original designs. However, papers in Leeds District Archives detailing plantings at Goldsborough, Yorkshire, include notes to the foreman showing Woods' vision of a margin of three to four feet in which to plant roses, jessamines and honeysuckles among flowers in front of short shrubs and evergreens backed with taller ones. Also planted in this sort of area were Portuguese laurels, *Arbutus*, Laurustinus (*Viburnum tinus*), 'Sistus', Chinese arborvita (*Thuja occidentalis*), and Sumachs, among others. Double-blossomed peaches, cherries and almonds, together with arborjudas (*Cercis siliquastrum*), tulip trees and thorns were used as flowering trees.[48]

Along the Lea at Brocket, the 1798 plan indicates plantings of what appear to be more shrubs and herbaceous plants, divided by snaking paths, leading north and south of a clearing containing a single specimen tree, which provided another route back to the walled garden area and the stables. A long building, with a projecting square bay at its south-west end, stood on the grassy knoll outside the first walled garden.

Below it, among the clumps of trees, was a small red square – an arbour or seat? Neither of these features exist now so it is difficult to conjecture on their use unless the former was perhaps the 'Temple'? The present 'Temple' is labelled as a Dairy on nineteenth-century Ordnance Survey maps and 1922 sale particulars[49] and was also referred to as the Dairy in

Figure 7.9 Detail of the 1798 estate plan, showing the planting alongside the river.
REPRODUCED BY KIND PERMISSION OF HALS (DE/P/P15)

the eighteenth-century accounts. This was an architectural dairy with marble basins and decorative plaster plaques on the walls (Figure 7.10), which served as an eye-catcher in the garden, comparable with the Dairy-Temple at Wardour.

The widened and remodelled stretch of the Broadwater extended to the edge of the park and had two islands at its north end, which would lead the eye to the simple Flint Bridge and the Fishing Arbour. A photograph of the latter appears on a postcard dated 1904, and shows a more decorative, turreted roofline than exists now (Figure 7.11). The arbour design is very similar to that shown on a plan for improvements at Wormsley, Buckinghamshire, drawn up in 1779.[50] Using a building or a bridge to mark where a river entered a park was another of Woods' favourite ploys.[51] This, and the use of grottoes to disguise the origin of an artificial river or lake, again show William Kent's influence. In some of Woods' landscapes the grotto led to a boathouse, while in others there was a seat placed above the arch. Here at Brocket the Fishing Arbour provided extra interest and no doubt housed a seat from which one could look back over the Broadwater to the Hall and down to Paine's bridge.

Kent designed landscapes with a painter's eye; his first profession was as an artist. His designs were inspired by Claude Lorraine's paintings. He used trees to frame vistas, cut off lower branches to allow a view through trees and produced many classically inspired buildings to

Figure 7.10 The Dairy at Brocket Park. PHOTOGRAPH BY KATE HARWOOD, 2006

enhance his landscapes. Woods, throughout his life, followed the more complicated and intricate landscape ideal of Kent, while Brown developed a much broader brushstroke, depending far more for his effects on sweeps of hills and swathes of woods.

Woods sited the two walled gardens on a gently rising slope above his riverside landscape (see Figure 7.9). The first garden is a typically 'Woodsian irregular shape'.[52] It is wide, with a shallow bay on the south side which would have collected the maximum sunlight and warmth. The river gate led to a wide path with two dipping ponds; a second wide path across the north side connected the east gate to the gardener's house, which was built in 1786 for £100. This is an attractive brick building with an apsidal end, which would have enhanced the appearance of the gardens, but was built after Woods' known involvement, although he could have left a design. The south-facing walls still have angle irons, ties and frames showing the extent of the fruit cases built on them. These were probably for peaches and cherries.

The main north–south path leads on up through another gate to the more northerly walled area which would appear to have a wider, grander glass house in the centre of its long range, facing down a central pathway leading back to the gardener's house. The remains of winding gear and ratchets for operating ventilation can still be found here. Two of the houses have arches in the walls denoting vineries. The 1922 sale

Figure 7.11 The Fishing Arbour, Brocket Park. PHOTOGRAPH BY ESTHER GATLAND, 2006

particulars list early and late vineries, a peach house and two fig houses –
probably unchanged since the nineteenth century.[53] On the 1798 map
both gardens have fruit trees against all the walls and trees surrounding
block planting in the beds. The overall effect would have been decorative
as well as productive. This was an extensive area with numerous
buildings and with a further open cultivated area outside the walls to the
north. This presumably grew the less decorative and more hardy crops.

Maintenance work in the garden and kitchen garden had separate
listings but both, until 1775, were entered under Farming expenses. The
pleasure garden is not listed as such until 1775 – the expenses for
hothouse and pinery occur here (not under kitchen garden), as does
North's bill of £26 17s for 'divers Shrubs and Trees'.[54] This supports the
idea of the walled garden being an integrated part of the pleasure garden.
There are no planting lists and carriage is listed more often than payment
for plants; 'divers things such as plants and shrubs', 'divers shrubs etc for
garden', and 'Garden Flowers', are not very enlightening or extensive. In
fact the plants noted as bought seem very sparse for such an extensive
enterprise – the walled gardens alone occupied six acres, according to the
1922 sale particulars. It may well be that much propagation was carried
out on-site, as was often the practice then, although one would expect
Woods to have ordered some of the choicer specimens or even supplied
them from his own nursery.

Woods designed rounded corners or apsidal ends in many of his
walled gardens. At Cannon Hall, Yorkshire, he had designed a hothouse
or pinery to stand outside the walls in a circle of grass, as a backdrop to a
flower garden; a similar arrangement is suggested by the red rectangular
structure shown on the 1798 plan of Brocket. He also placed a circle of
grass in front of the hothouse at Cannon Hall, to 'be richly adorned with
the choicest flowers and exoticks etc'.[55] In a similar vein, in the second
walled garden at Brocket are what seem to be two circles of grass in front
of the wall of hothouses, surrounded by lines of small trees bordering
paths. Apparently new cultivated beds were still being created in the
walled gardens after Woods' departure, as a relatively large sum (£6 8s)
was spent on asparagus roots in December 1777.[56] In 1785, carriage of
13s was paid for bringing a case of pine plants from the Duke of
Portland's estate at Welbeck Abbey, Nottinghamshire.[57] This is a little late
to have created a dedicated pinery as pineapples were no longer such a
novelty by then, but they could have been replacements. The garden

created by Woods at Hartwell, Buckinghamshire, was half productive and half ornamental, while that at Hatfield Peverel, Essex, showed the same elements as at Brocket, although on a different scale – pleasure garden following the winding bank of the river allied to a walled garden with a combination of kitchen garden and pleasure garden.

The design for an alcove seat for Wardour in 1765[58] (or something similar) may have been carried out at Brocket, where a narrow red structure is shown on the brow of the Templehill plantation on the 1798 plan (Figure 7.12). It would appear that Woods re-employed designs on several occasions in similar circumstances (the alcove seat reappears on the plan for Hengrave, Suffolk, in 1777). This seat would have overlooked Paine's bridge and the cascade. Woods' practice might have been to plant 'chiefly evergreens, except some larches, laburnums and weeping willows' near the cascade, as he advised at Cusworth, Yorkshire.[59] A planting plan for the mount at Goldsborough, Yorkshire, specified oaks, elms, beech and chestnuts, interspersed with flowering cherries, tulip trees, thorns and filberts, all of which backed a seat on the mount. This mount was in a more sheltered area next to the old kitchen garden – the planting at Brocket would have been in a more exposed site, on a natural eminence. Pallett's map shows a double line of sheltering and partially encircling trees – twelve in all – looking like conifers. If the seat was wooden, it would explain the lack of any surviving footprint now.

Figure 7.12 Detail of the 1798 estate plan showing the seat and Templehill plantation (left) overlooking the bridge and cascade (right). REPRODUCED BY KIND PERMISSION OF HALS (DE/P/P15)

One enigma of Brocket is the group of imposing swamp cypresses by the river. They were first introduced from North America by Tradescant the Younger but were probably not established here until much later. Woods did not use them anywhere else.[60] However, they are of a considerable size – the largest was 105 feet tall with a girth of 12.5 feet in 1976. This compares with a tree from the oldest recorded planting, which was at Syon House, Middlesex, in 1750. This tree was 105 feet tall with a girth of 13 feet in 1976 – so they could be a similar age.[61] William Lamb's game book carries a detailed record of the trees planted in the park from 1793 to 1823 and there is no entry of *Taxodium distichum* during this period.[62] Trees do grow at different rates in different sites (which have different soil conditions and experience different climates) and, in 1991, only one of the Brocket trees had developed the knee-like growths, called pneumatophores, which this species produces as a response to the waterlogged soil in its natural swampy habitat.[63] This suggests that the growing conditions in Brocket Park are perhaps not ideal. Probably the only way to settle their planting date will be a count of growth rings when the next tree falls.

Postscript

It might almost seem that Brocket had been redesigned for its most important role in the nineteenth century as the home of two of Britain's prime ministers. William Lamb inherited the estate in 1828 and must have taken consolation, after his electoral defeat in 1841, when he was host to Queen Victoria during her tour of Whig houses. Visits to Woburn and Panshanger were followed by a visit to Brocket with Emily, William's sister, acting as hostess. After lunch for thirty-six in the ballroom, William, his hair streaming in the wind, took the Queen on his arm round the lawn to show her the 'amphitheatre of heads' – a crowd up to the rails and spreading up the hill – while the Welwyn band played. She was then conducted round the house and on a circuit of the grounds, covering the shrubbery, greenhouse, hothouse and melon ground (probably outside the walls), back through the shrubbery and round by the water house. Brocket was apparently the chief delight of the three houses for her, because it was Melbourne's home. The Queen told Emily's daughter, 'William did the honours of the house exceeding well'.[64]

This tour of the gardens illustrates Woods' coherent vision of the integration of the productive and the decorative aspects of the walled garden with the river landscape. The wide gateway from the second walled area to the shrubbery area has very striking carved stone gateposts, a lion to the right and a dragon to the left, which also suggests that this was part of a pleasure circuit.

Peniston Lamb entertained most of the leading racing fraternity, including the Prince Regent, and the Racing Calendar of 1799 shows races there from 2 to 4 May, featuring the best horses of the day. Two sweepstakes were advertised for 1800. The subscription list was headed by His Royal Highness, the Duke of Bedford and the Lords Egremont, Clarendon and Burford. Entertainments were apparently long and lavish around racing days.[65] Pete Wilkerson's *Racing in Hertfordshire* (Hertford, 2002) refers to the Prince Regent always attending, as well as Sir John Shelley, Sir Charles Bunbury and other leading men of the turf. The racecourse sits well in the park layout (see Plate 7.5), despite being laid out (at the Prince Regent's suggestion) after Woods had left, and parts of it are now followed by keen golfers. Woods' design has proved adaptable.

Emily Lamb had initially married the sixth Earl Cowper of nearby Panshanger and, after his death, married Lord Palmerston in 1839. Emily eventually inherited Brocket and so it became the home of a second prime minister.

Figure 7.13 An imposing gateway between the walled gardens and the riverside shrubbery.
PHOTOGRAPH BY ESTHER GATLAND, 2006

Whether or not you agree wholeheartedly with Tipping's assessment, the charm of Brocket lies largely in its setting – this is to a great extent Woods' achievement. Interestingly, it is only at Brocket and Wardour that Woods' planting in the wider landscape is both acknowledged and praised, in the late eighteenth century and the twentieth. Two of these comments include the word picturesque and, although this is given a small 'p', Woods did once venture into the Picturesque – at Wynnstay in North Wales.[66] Perhaps, as Richard Bisgrove comments, the fashion for the style of Kent and his followers might have returned at the turn of the eighteenth century (as a reaction to Brown's landscapes), but for the veritable explosion of plants available to gardeners which led to the plants themselves assuming more importance than the overall design.[67]

The print in Figure 7.14, from Angus' *Seats of the Nobility*, shows a Chinese boat on the Broadwater. He tells us the boat was originally 'the property of Benjamin Trueman, the Building of which took three hundred pounds'. It would certainly have added atmosphere to the Broadwater vista, in the manner of the Duke of Cumberland's 'pagoda-roofed' Chinese junk on Virginia Water.[68]

Figure 7.14 Brocket Hall, by Paul Sandby for W. Angus, 1787. REPRODUCED BY KIND PERMISSION OF HALS (DE/X55/Z2/12)

Acknowledgements

I would like to acknowledge the generosity of Fiona Cowell in allowing me to refer at length to her elegant, but as yet unpublished, thesis on Richard Woods.

Notes

1. A. Tipping, 'Brocket Hall', *Country Life*, 58 (1925), p. 98.
2. D. Stroud, *Capability Brown* (London, 1957).
3. H. Prince, *Parks in England* (Somerset, 1967); D. Jacques, *Georgian gardens* (London, 1983); F. Cowell, 'Richard Woods, A preliminary account', *Garden History*, 14 (1986), pp. 85–119; *Garden History*, 15 (1987), pp. 19–54, 115–135; 'Richard Woods', (PhD thesis, University of East Anglia, 2005).
4. Cowell attributes the difficulties of ascertaining dates and details of his birth, education and first marriage to the fact that he was a Catholic living in penal times.
5. Cowell, 'Preliminary account' (1986), pp. 85–119.
6. F. Cowell, 'Richard Woods', Prelim Acc Part II, p. 38.
7. Cowell, 'Preliminary account' (1987), p. 117.
8. *Ibid.*, p. 115.
9. *Ibid.*, p. 124.
10. J. Phibbs, *Assassination of Capability Brown* (paper for the AGT and GHS, 1994)
11. R. Bisgrove, *The English garden* (London, 1990), p. 106.
12. D. Stuart, *The plants that shaped our gardens* (London, 2002), pp. 40, 46–52.
13. M. Laird, *The flowering of the landscape garden* (Philadelphia, 1999).
14. T. Williamson, *Polite Landscapes* (Stroud, 1995).
15. Cowell, 'Preliminary account' (1987), p. 116.
16. Cowell, 'Richard Woods', Gazetteer p. 267.
17. HALS, A. Dury and J. Andrews, *A topographical map of Hartford-Shire* (1766; republished by the Hertfordshire Record Society in 2004).
18. HALS, DE/Ry/P3, Map of Manor and Lands of Newsells, 1788 (no surveyor).
19. HALS, DE/Ry/P5, Plan of New Park in County of Herts, seat of John Peachey, 1791; HALS DZ/65/Z1, Book of Reference; HALS DE/Ry/P6, Plan of New Park and home farm, no surveyor, *c*.1791.
20. Ordnance Survey map sheet XXVIII.10, 25 inches to the mile, 1881.
21. Cowell, 'Richard Woods', p. 117.
22. *Ibid.*, Gazetteer p. 267.
23. Reproduced in P. Hobhouse, *Plants in the English Landscape* (London, 1992), p. 215.
24. HALS, DZ/65/Z3, notes on Newsells – house, chapel, grotto and icehouse.
25. HALS, County Views Collection, BARK/49a–c, sketches of hermitage, font and holy-water stoop.
26. Cowell, 'Richard Woods', pp. 175–81 has a full discussion of Woods' kitchen garden shapes.
27. HALS, DE/Ry/P5; HALS DZ/65/Z1.
28. J. Spence (J.M. Osborn, ed.), *Observations, anecdotes, and characters of books and men* (Oxford, 1966).
29. HALS, DE/Ry/P6.
30. Winnington is shown with Stephen and Henry Fox, Lord Hervey, and the Duke of Marlborough in Hogarth's *The Holland House Group*, 1738, hanging at Ickworth, Suffolk, reproduced as a postcard by the National Trust.
31. P. Willis, *Charles Bridgeman and the English landscape* (Newcastle on Tyne, 2002), p. 87. The plan is held at the Bodleian Library: Gough a.3 fo.7 and a.4 fo.40. A payment was made by Winnington to Bridgeman's widow.
32. R. King, *The quest for paradise* (Weybridge, 1979), p. 180.
33. HALS, DE/P/P9, Brocket Hall and Warren Farm, 1752, surveyor unknown.

34. P. Leach, *James Paine* (London, 1988).
35. J. Harris, *The artist and the country house* (London, 1979), p. 294.
36. Cowell, 'Richard Woods' (2005), Gazetteer p. 46.
37. D. Cecil, *The young Melbourne* (Toronto, 1939).
38. Anon., *Copper Plate Magazine*, 2, pl. 76 (1793–4).
39. Cowell quoting W. Angus, *Seats of the Nobility* (Islington, 1787), Prelim Acc Part II, p. 27.
40. Cowell, 'Richard Woods', p. 34.
41. HALS, 63828, Account book of the estates of Lord Melbourne, 1772–1791.
42. Prior to decimalisation, there were 20 shillings (s) to the pound (£) and 12 pennies (d) to the shilling. Therefore a shilling was worth 5p and there were 2.4d to a decimal penny (p).
43. HALS, DE/P/P15, *Survey of Brocket Park* by Thomas Pallett, 1798. There are two other versions of this map (not held at HALS), one reproduced in *Country Life*, 1925, the other reproduced on the cover of the 1991 Cass Surveys and proposals.
44. Tipping, 'Brocket Hall', pp. 98–100.
45. Paine's plan is reproduced in Tipping's article in *Country Life*, 1925.
46. Cowell, 'Preliminary account' (1987), pp. 124–5.
47. Quoted in Cowell, 'Richard Woods', p. 67.
48. Leeds District Archives, TN/EA19/1, Goldsborough, Yorkshire. Memo to foreman, Wm Stone, 1764. (I am indebted to Kate Harwood for obtaining a copy of this for my use.)
49. HALS, H50 598 3088, Brocket Hall Sale Catalogue, 1922.
50. Cowell, 'Preliminary account' (1987), p. 125.
51. The grotto/boathouse at Cusworth, Yorkshire, is remarkably similar to the Flint Bridge at Brocket.
52. Cowell, 'Richard Woods', Gazetteer p. 47.
53. HALS, H50 598 3088.
54. HALS, 63828.
55. Cowell, 'Preliminary account' (1987), pp. 119, 124.
56. HALS, 63828.
57. *Ibid.*
58. Cowell, 'Preliminary account' (1987), p. 118.
59. *Ibid.*, p. 124.
60. Fiona Cowell, pers. comm.
61. Cass Associates, Landscape Survey, development strategy and planning proposals (1991), p. 34.
62. HALS, DE/Lb/F52, William Lamb's Game Book, 1793–1823.
63. Cass Associates, Landscape Survey, p. 34.
64. P. Zeigler, *Melbourne, a biography of William Lamb* (London, 1976), p. 339.
65. W.M. Torrens, *Memoirs of Lord Melbourne* (London, 1890), p. 28.
66. Cowell, 'Richard Woods', p. 215.
67. Bisgrove, *The English garden*, p. 105.
68. T. Mowl, *Gentlemen and players, gardeners of the English landscape* (Stroud, 2000), p. 123.

Bibliography

Primary sources

Bodleian Library, Oxford, Gough a3 fo.7 and a4 fo.40

Hertfordshire Archives and Local Studies (hereafter HALS), 63828, Account book of the estates of Lord Melbourne audited by John Thompson, 1772–1791

HALS, BARK/49a–c, sketches of hermitage, font and holy-water stoop

HALS, DE/Bg/2/112, painting of Newsells by J.C. Buckler, c.1840

HALS, DE/Lb/F52, William Lamb's Game Book, 1793–1823

HALS, DE/P/P9, Brocket Hall and Warren Farm, 1752, surveyor unknown

HALS, DE/P/P15, Survey of Brocket Park by Thomas Pallett, 1798

HALS, DE/Ry/P3, Map of Manor and Lands of Newsells, 1788 (no surveyor)

HALS, DE/Ry/P6, Plan of New Park and home farm, no surveyor, c.1791

HALS, DE/Ry/P5, Plan of New Park in County of Herts, seat of John Peachey, 1791

HALS, DE/X55/Z2/12, illustration of Brocket Hall by P. Sandby for W. Angus, 1787

HALS, DE/X55/Z2/13–14, drawing of Brocket Park by E.F. Burney, 1786

HALS, Dury, A. and Andrews, J., *A topographical map of Hartford-Shire* (1766; republished by the Hertfordshire Record Society in 2004)

HALS, DZ/65/Z1, Book of Reference for 1788 survey of Newsells

HALS, DZ/65/Z3, notes on Newsells – house, chapel, grotto and icehouse

HALS, H50 598 3088, Brocket Hall Sale Catalogue, 1922

HALS, HAT/30, illustration of Brocket Hall by J.C. Carter, c.1800–50

Leeds District Archives, TN/EA19/1, Goldsborough, Yorkshire, Memo to foreman, Wm Stone, 1764

Secondary sources

Anon., *Copper Plate Magazine*, 2, pl. 76 (1793–4)

Angus, W., *Seats of the Nobility* (Islington, 1787), pl.2

Bisgrove, R., *The English garden* (London, 1990)

Cass Associates, *Landscape Survey, development strategy and planning proposals* (1991)

Cecil, D., *The young Melbourne* (Toronto, 1939)

Cowell, F., 'Richard Woods, A preliminary account', *Garden History*, 14 (1986)

Cowell, F., 'Richard Woods, A preliminary account', *Garden History*, 15 (1987)

Cowell, F., 'Richard Woods', (PhD thesis, University of East Anglia, 2005)

Harris, J., *The artist and the country house* (London, 1979)

Hobhouse, P., *Plants in garden history* (London, 1992)

Jacques, D., *Georgian gardens* (London, 1983)

King, R., *The quest for paradise* (Weybridge, 1979)

Laird, M., *The flowering of the landscape garden* (Philadelphia, 1999)

Leach, P., *James Paine* (London, 1988)

Mowl, T., *Gentlemen and players, gardeners of the English landscape* (Stroud, 2000)

Phibbs, J., *Assassination of Capability Brown* (paper for the AGT and GHS, 1994)

Prince, H., *Parks in England* (Somerset, 1967)

Spence, J., (Osborn, J.M., ed.), *Observations, anecdotes, and characters of books and men* (Oxford, 1966)

Stroud, D., *Capability Brown* (London, 1957)

Stuart, D., *The plants that shaped our gardens* (London, 2002)

Tipping, A., 'Brocket Hall', *Country Life*, 58 (1925)

Torrens, W.M., *Memoirs of Lord Melbourne* (London, 1890)

Wilkerson, P., *Racing in Hertfordshire* (Hertford, 2002)

Williamson, T., *Polite landscapes* (Stroud, 1995)

Willis, P., *Charles Bridgeman and the English landscape* (Newcastle on Tyne, 2002)

Zeigler, P., *Melbourne, a biography of William Lamb* (London, 1976)

CHAPTER EIGHT

The Pulham family of Hertfordshire and their work

Kate Banister

In the pretty and pleasant village of Broxbourne, reached by the Eastern Counties Railway, and distant nineteen miles from the Metropolis, there is a small, but very interesting, manufactory of works in terra-cotta to which we desire to conduct our readers.[1]

This is the opening sentence in an article in the prestigious *Art-Journal* for 1859. It refers to the firm of James Pulham, soon to be Pulham and Sons. Later well known for the manufacture of cement, artificial rocks and stoneware, the firm had been established in London in 1820 by William Lockwood, who installed the first James Pulham as manager. Some twenty years later the firm, under the chairmanship of the second James Pulham, moved to Broxbourne, to the above-mentioned 'manufactory'. Here vases, urns and garden ornaments were made in clay-based and cement-based artificial stone. By the 1880s, probably at the height of their success, James Pulham and Sons were making garden ornaments and furniture, building rockeries and ferneries in natural stone or Pulhamite (artificial stone), and, by the end of the century, they were advertising themselves as garden landscapers, skilled not only in water gardens, but Dutch, Italian and Japanese styles as well.[2] In 1895 they received the Royal Warrant from the then Prince of Wales, which was continued on his accession to the throne as King Edward VII, and was also granted by King George V. Up to the time of the First World War they were involved in the design of several notable gardens, including those at Buckingham Palace and the Royal Horticultural Society's Surrey home at Wisley. However, the effect of two world wars on gardening and general prosperity led to the closure of the family business in 1945.

Unfortunately, documentary evidence for both the family and the firm is scant. All official records were lost when the firm closed down: all we have are a few copies of the promotional booklet, entitled *Picturesque Ferneries and Rock-Garden Scenery*, written and produced by the second James Pulham in 1876/7.[3] However, this does include a list of the places where 'the Pulhamite System of forming Rocks' had been installed in the previous twenty-eight years. This shows that from 1849 the firm was working all over the country, and not just locally in Hertfordshire, London and the south-east. A few copies of a trade catalogue survive, but these date from the early years of the twentieth century and do not give an exhaustive list of the firm's products.[4] Some of the gardens on which the firm worked have been known for many years and, as might be expected, of these some are in a better state than others. However, evidence of new gardens is constantly being uncovered, of which Dewstow (near Monmouth), with its spectacular grottoes and tunnels, is an outstanding example. English Heritage is in the process of producing guidelines for the care and restoration of Pulhamite (artificial) rocks in gardens, and sales catalogues of antique garden furniture show the huge prices that the terracotta items now fetch. As for archaeological evidence, in 1986 Broxbourne Borough Council decided to restore what remained of the manufactory, including the brick kiln and puddling wheel, used to grind the claystone (Figures 8.1 and 8.2). The site is now listed and officially maintained.

There were four generations of Pulham involved in the firm and, in each case, the eldest son was called James.[5] The first James was born in 1788 in Woodbridge, Suffolk. He was one of a large, poor family: the children received no formal education. James, however, attended evening classes and, with his brother Obadiah, was apprenticed to John and William Lockwood, the principal builder in Woodbridge. In fact, he showed such promise as a modeller that he was quickly promoted to foreman over some thirty employees. It was he who, now eighteen years of age, was responsible for making the tower and mouldings of 'The Castle', a mansion William Lockwood had built for himself. The aim was to demonstrate the advantages of Roman cement (for which the Lockwoods were an agency). This was used for the roof, battlements and window mouldings and also as a covering for the whole building, which was then colour washed. The mouldings were first made in pipe-clay; then casts were taken in plaster or cement made on the premises. James

Figure 8.1 Kiln from the Pulham manufactory at Broxbourne. PHOTOGRAPH BY ANNE ROWE, 2000

Figure 8.2 Puddling wheel from the Pulham manufactory at Broxbourne. PHOTOGRAPH BY
ANNE ROWE, 2000

Figure 8.6 Pulham Fountain, 1862. REPRODUCED BY KIND PERMISSION OF CITY OF WESTMINSTER LIBRARIES (*ART-JOURNAL*, 1862, p. 162)

Figure 8.7 Mulready monument in Kensal Green Cemetery. PHOTOGRAPH BY KATE BANISTER, 2004

Figure 8.8 Ruins and grotto at Woodlands, Hoddesdon, *c*.1910. REPRODUCED BY KIND PERMISSION OF LOWEWOOD MUSEUM, BROXBOURNE BOROUGH

Figure 8.9 Façade of the Orangery, formerly part of the gardens at Woodlands, Hoddesdon. PHOTOGRAPH BY KATE BANISTER, 2006

Kensington Museum (later to be known as the Victoria and Albert Museum) for the *Exposition Universelle* in Paris in 1867. A life-size effigy of the painter rests on a raised bier and on the square pedestal at the base are reliefs illustrating some of his works. The whole is covered by a canopy supported by columns. Well-preserved and easily accessible, it is now in Kensal Green Cemetery, marking the grave of the painter (Figure 8.7). Of more local interest is the memorial to Charlotte Annie, sister-in-law of James Pulham, in Cheshunt Cemetery. Erected in 1890, it is a standing angel, with fine drapery and one arm raised above the head (Plate 8.4). The *c*.1920 Pulham catalogue shows a continuing line of vases and fountains but, gradually, the repertoire came to include seats, balustrades, sundials, bird baths, pergolas and the layout of whole gardens in the fashionable styles of the time. Unfortunately not all the terracotta items were stamped and, in the absence of catalogues earlier than the twentieth century, it is difficult to be certain about the provenance of any item. When gardens in which they were placed fell into disrepair, the furniture was often vandalised or stolen.

Probably one of the earliest gardens in Hertfordshire that Pulham worked on was that at Woodlands, Hoddesdon, for John Warner. The list in *Picturesque Ferneries and Rock-Garden Scenery* mentions three years (1839, 1849 and 1862) and itemises a waterfall and a fernery.[14] Photographs show ruins and a grotto and it is tempting to assume Pulham had a hand in these too (Figure 8.8). The *Gardeners' Chronicle* of 1842 describes huge pieces of granite which had the appearance of having braved a thousand winters, although they had been completed only a few months. The article goes on – 'in reality it is composed of large blocks of artificial stone, formed of brick rubbish and clinker, over which a cement mixture was poured and then moulded into shape'.[15] In addition, there was a fountain (also described in the *Gardeners' Chronicle*) which might well have been made by Pulham. In fact, there were seven fountains in the garden. Certainly the ornate decoration on the façade of the Orangery was found, on restoration, to have been made by the firm. Little now remains of this garden: the lake is in the grounds of the Hoddesdon Civic Centre and the Orangery has been converted to a private house (Figure 8.9). The rest of the garden is now under the Police Station.

The firm became Pulham and Son in 1865, when the third James joined it at the age of twenty. A study of the list in the booklet shows that in 1876/7, the date of its publication and some thirty years after the establishment of the firm in Broxbourne, only six of the properties listed were in Hertfordshire. The firm was building rock gardens (using both natural stone, if available, as well as their own concoctions) and ferneries all over the country. In the garden of his London home in Tottenham, James constructed a 'rocky-cliff' to show what might be done 'for picturesque effect' to make a rock garden 'pleasing all the year round, including the dull days of autumn and winter'.[16] He died here in 1898, but is buried in Broxbourne churchyard. A rock wall created from Pulhamite at Bedwell Park (Essendon) in 1866 is still a spectacular feature (Plate 8.5) and the fernery at Danesbury (Welwyn) remains reasonably intact. However, of the other early Pulham gardens in Hertfordshire – Bayfordbury and Poles Park near Ware (see Figure 8.13) – little remains of their former glory. From the 1880s onwards, when the fashion for rockeries and ferneries was beginning to exhaust itself, Pulham and Sons, from their London offices, directed operations all over Great Britain and Northern Ireland, building water gardens and designing Italianate features and fashionable garden furniture. No detailed list of larger contracts after 1877 survives, so information about their later commissions has to be pieced together from contemporary magazines and estate records.

Figure 8.10 Pulham bridge at Aldenham House *c.* 1900. REPRODUCED BY KIND PERMISSION OF LORD ALDENHAM (HABERDASHERS' ASKE'S SCHOOL LIBRARY, ALDENHAM ARCHIVE)

Of their later landscape work in Hertfordshire three examples survive, of which one is freely open to the public. Carpenders Park, Watford, is now the site of the local cemetery but along the stream which bounds the site is an ornamental bridge (now much overgrown), a waterfall (Figure 8.12) and other landscaped features. These are in an area called Woodwalks, which was part of the estate bought by Robert Russell Carew in 1862. Aldenham House, now the Haberdashers' Aske's School, became the home of the Gibbs family in 1868 and meticulous records were kept of the alterations to the house and estate. Edwin Beckett, the head gardener for forty-eight years, also took over 500 photographs, which form a unique record of a garden that was said to be the rival of Kew in its collection of trees. Fifty-eight gardeners looked after the estate, which included a kitchen garden and orchard. In the 1890s Henry Hucks Gibbs called in Pulham and Sons to lay out water gardens. Figure 8.10 shows Edwin Beckett (in the boater) on the little bridge. Originally the land was flat and of London clay but Pulham built channels for water to run through a series of pools, under two bridges and over a waterfall, flowing ultimately into a swimming pool.[17] The bridges and rocks are of artificial stone. Very similar bridges can be seen in the gardens of Buckingham Palace – of basic brick construction, coated with cement and moulded to resemble old stone. The Node, Codicote, is mentioned in the *Gardeners' Magazine* of 1912 as another site of Pulham's work. Here, they constructed a terraced garden, which survives today, together with rockwork around a large pool and a rockwork arch. A photograph of the pergola appears in the trade catalogue of *c*.1925.

The Gardeners' Magazine of 1912 has a column about the third James, who was 'ably assisted by his sons'.[18] A short list of their work is given and it includes Waddesdon (Buckinghamshire), Sandringham (Norfolk), where they constructed a lake and a boathouse (for which they received a Royal Warrant), Buckingham Palace and Wisley (Surrey). Here, above the ponds, a large tank was built at the top of the bank to supply the water, and hundreds of tons of Sussex sandstone (they now worked increasingly in natural stone) were brought in and arranged in blocks, with waterfalls and pools descending the slope. 'It seems natural for everyone who visits Wisley to go first to see the rock-garden' said the *Gardeners' Chronicle* in 1920.[19] The third James died this same year.

Not all the Pulhams' rockwork was for private individuals. The early nineteenth century saw the movement for public parks as places for exercise and refreshment in the cities. The most well-known of these in which the firm was involved was Battersea Park (1866–70). Here, to screen the view of Clapham Railway Station from the lake, huge artificial rocks were piled up on level ground to create a mountainous scene, complete with waterfall and a stream. At Preston, too, they built rocks and waterfalls (1860–90). At Ramsgate, in the last decade of the nineteenth century, they were contracted by the local authorities to build rockwork gardens to attract the summer visitors, and at Folkestone huge cliff walls were built either side of an existing coastal path. Mrs Festing also mentions possibly the first instance of Pulham work abroad – a waterfall and tunnel in Gisselfeld Park, Denmark (1894).[20]

There were many reasons for the success of the firm lasting for over 100 years. First must come the quality of their work. In his promotional booklet the second James gives tantalising hints of his knowledge and education. He thought it essential to have not just 'practical experience in the most various cements', but also to have some architectural knowledge ('I was brought up as an architectural modeller, succeeding my father').[21] It was reading *Phillip's Geology* and *Glimpses of the Ancient Earth* that gave him his love of geology and led him to making 'rocks'.[22]

Figure 8.11 Unknown female in rock garden. REPRODUCED BY KIND PERMISSION OF THE RHS LINDLEY LIBRARY (J. PULHAM, *PICTURESQUE FERNERIES AND ROCK-GARDEN SCENERY,* p. 13)

These rocks were not just thrown together – not only was the base material thoroughly covered, but the surface was fingered, tooled and brushed to make the finished effect more convincing. And durability was guaranteed. 'Rocks' were spectacularly tilted to imitate geological faults; streams were diverted, ponds drained and water fed through cemented trenches to feed cascades and water gardens. 'It is difficult to believe that man has had any hand in its arrangement and construction,' wrote the *Gardeners' Chronicle* of Madresfield (near Malvern).[23] Indeed, some experts were taken in: Sir Robert Murchison, an eminent naturalist, was deceived by the rocks at Lockinge (Berkshire) and declared them to be of the same stone as the church. One of the most appealing pictures in the booklet illustrates Pulham's idea of a natural arch formed by a fissure in rocks (Figure 8.11). He gives us no clue who the lady in the hat and muff is, nor of the location of the garden (if indeed it existed), but the rocks, ferns and birch tree all demonstrate Pulham's intention to produce naturalistic rockwork.

Nor was he without knowledge and advice on the most suitable plants for his rock gardens and ferneries. The rocks should have pockets where moisture could collect for the 'well-being' of plants. Water might well have to be introduced as an accompaniment to rocks – hence his dropping-wells, although he was well aware of the discomfort of sitting in damp and uninviting caves. He included a list of suitable plants, advocated a judicious mixture of variegated and evergreen foliage and recommended William Robinson's *Alpine flowers for English gardens* as an instructive and interesting guide. Quite clearly Alpine flowers were new at this time and the Pulhams were keen to encourage the fashion.

As employers the Pulhams valued their workforce and relied on them to maintain the quality and high standards of their products. 'A staff of men have been instructed and grown up in the work'.[24] Practical knowledge of various cements was essential. The 1871 census lists forty men and nine boys in the factory at Broxbourne – not that substantial, considering the work they were doing at the time, but the policy was: 'Mr Pulham aimed more at quality than quantity, and it is said he still carries out the rule he laid down, not to extend his business, but to keep it so that it is not too large to be under his own personal supervision'.[25] In a footnote Pulham explained that his terracotta 'helps to keep the workforce employed in winter, when much cannot be done during severe weather, and it keeps our men together through many years, as many have been in our employ twenty years, some more'.[26] Clearly a loyal and experienced workforce was essential to the success of the firm. There was no shortage of satisfied clients from all walks of life and parts of the country.

Another reason for the Pulhams' success was the contemporary interest in rocks and ferns, an interest which the second James clearly shared. (His booklet contains a poem of twenty-six verses to describe a Pulhamite Fernery or Winter Garden!) Loudon, in his *Encyclopaedia of Gardening*, speaks of 'the grandeur of rocks', sometimes mixed with the 'singular, fantastic or romantic'.[27] Pulham frequently mentions the 'rugged, picturesque' effect of a scene, and he names actual places (such as Cumberland, Westmoreland, Wales, Devon and Scotland) where natural rocks could be enjoyed and copied in gardens. He even quotes Byron, adding two lines of his own to support his view, and shows an almost evangelical zeal to have rockwork created in the correct way – 'rugged, irregular and of varied outline ... to form a striking feature ... and lend enchantment to the view'.[28] The Sublime and the Picturesque of the late eighteenth and early nineteenth century were still part of some contemporary aesthetic ideals. Accordingly, Pulham was quick to criticise what he called the prevalent 'Cockney tea-garden style' of rockeries – adorned with glass, clinkers, spar, flints, etc.[29]

Along with rockwork went an interest in follies – ancient towers and ruins and gateways, as at Benington. Pulham's list includes a Fairy Cave built in 1873 for the Earl of Stradbrooke at Henham Hall (Suffolk) and, at Denmark Hill (1869–71), a Moorish Temple in the rock, highly decorated in colours and gold.

Of the 166 places mentioned in Pulham's list of 1876/7, nearly two-thirds are ferneries; for this was the time when fern collecting was at its height. The fernery at Danesbury, Welwyn, was specifically mentioned by William Robinson in his *The English Flower Garden* of 1883. These ferneries varied from just a wall at the end of a conservatory (as at Woodlands, Hoddesdon, for the Warners) to one built at the side of a hill or even in an unused quarry. As with all their garden designs the Pulhams were more concerned with taste and method of construction than size. So a miniature fernery could be made from a 'rockified' wall planted with 'mementoes of a favourite spot'[30] or a more elaborate Ferndelabrum – a series of basins one above another in a space five or six feet square. Or a fern case, fitted with a moderate quantity of tufa rock in the window, could sometimes hide an unsightly view of a blank wall. Pulham tufa work

Figure 8.12 Examples of the range of work produced by the Pulham manufactory: the bridge over Spitalbrook, Hoddesdon; rockwork at Carpenders Park; a mask from the wall of dining-hall at Benington Lordship; a terracotta vase, pedestal and decorative wall coping. PHOTOGRAPHS BY KATE BANISTER, 2006 AND ANNE ROWE, 2000

survives in the fernery at The Swiss Garden, Old Warden, Bedfordshire.

Pulham and Sons had, and still have, their detractors – the booklet refers to the House of Commons debate in 1870 when so-called gentlemen of taste ridiculed their artificial rocks in Battersea Park. What was being criticised was not the quality of the work, but the principle of making fake rocks. However, in the 1990s, when suppliers of garden stonework were removing large quantities of limestone from the countryside and thereby threatening the ecology of the limestone pavements, an eminent geologist recommended a return to artificial stone as made by Pulham.[31] But the 'old-established firm of Messrs Pulham & Sons'[32] could not survive the huge changes brought about by two world wars: the staff who were needed to look after huge gardens did not exist any more, and years of austerity spelled the end of lavish expense on horticultural fashions. However, the durability of the materials and the thoroughness of the execution has ensured that beneath the overgrown foliage there still lie examples of Pulham rockwork and terracotta furniture waiting to be discovered.

Known sites of Pulham work in Hertfordshire:
(Note the concentration of sites near the manufactory in Broxbourne)

1835/7 **Benington Lordship** for George Proctor
Gateway, dining-hall and summerhouse forming a courtyard: all of flint with artificial stone dressings, mouldings and windows; 'built as a ruin, supposed to be real' (Pulham 1876/7, p. 38)
Open to the public on certain days of the year (01438 86966; www.beningtonlordship.co.uk)

1838, 1849, 1862 **Woodlands, Hoddesdon** for John Warner
Waterfall and fernery
Site now occupied by the Civic Hall and the Police Station
Nothing remains of this garden except the lake in the grounds of the Civic Hall and the converted Orangery

1845 **Bayfordbury, Hertford** for William Robert Baker
Rose gardens, rock gardens, pool and fountains
Little surviving Pulham work
Private property: no public access

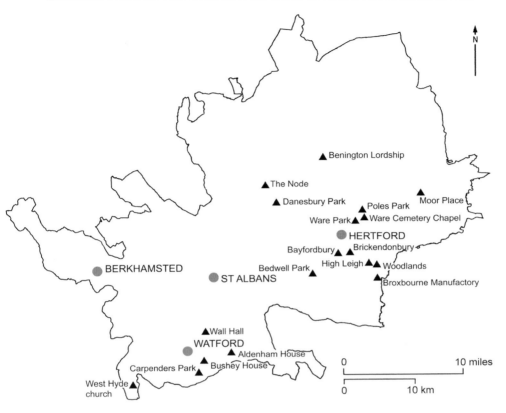

Figure 8.13 Map of known Pulham sites in Hertfordshire. © ANNE ROWE

1843/5 St Thomas' church, West Hyde
Flint building with cement dressings and plaster angels on the interior of the roof
In regular use as a parish church

1854 Ware cemetery chapel
'Pulham' stamp on base of pillars
No longer in use as a chapel

1859/60 Danesbury Park, Welwyn for W.J. Blake Esq.
Cave, dropping-well and pass, in a chalk pit, for growth of ferns and other rock plants; of artificial stone
Dilapidated remains
Private property: no public access

1865/6 **Poles Park, Ware** for R. Hanbury Esq.
Conservatory with fernery at one end and a dropping-well; rose garden and fountain
Little survives
Now owned by the Marriott Hanbury Manor Hotel: access to guests

1866 **Bedwell Park** for R.C. Hanbury Esq., MP
Fernery, cliffs to hide a wall and enclose a root-house for ferns, rock plants and shrubs
Private property: no public access

c.1875 **High Leigh, Hoddesdon** for Robert Barclay
Rock garden, waterfall, grotto and folly arch
Private property: no public access

1876 **Aldenham Abbey (now Wall Hall), Aldenham** for F. Durham
Fernery
Private property: no public access

1880 **Ware Park, Hertford** for William Parker
Rock garden, summerhouse and folly arch
Private property: no public access

1891 **Carpenders Park, Watford** for Robert Russell Carew
Rockwork, bridge and cascade
Part of civil cemetery: open to the public

1892/7 **Aldenham House, Elstree** for Henry Hucks Gibbs
Water gardens, bridges and a pool
Now the Haberdashers' Aske's School: no public access

1911 **The Node, Codicote** for Lord Brocket and, later, Carl Holmes
Rose garden, terrace, sunken garden and rockwork
Private property: no public access

Additional (recently discovered) sites of Pulham work:

c.1900 Bushey House, Bushey, Watford
Ornamental water course, wall with balustrading and bastions
Private care home for the elderly: no public access

Moor Place, Much Hadham (date of Pulham work unknown)
Pergola, pond borders with planting pockets
Private property: garden occasionally open for charity

after 1902 Brickendonbury, Hertford
Rock garden with cascade
Private property: no public access

Acknowledgements
My thanks go to: Claude Hitching, who is writing a book on the Pulhams and has a very informative website, www.pulham.org.uk; the Curator and Staff of Lowewood Museum, Hoddesdon; Mr and Mrs R. Bott of Benington Lordship; Keith Cheyney and the Headmaster of Haberdashers' Aske's School; Lord Aldenham; the Vicar and Churchwardens of West Hyde Church; Anne Rowe; RHS Lindley Library; and City of Westminster Libraries.

Notes
1. Anon., *Art-Journal* (1859), p. 25.
2. 'Pulhamite' is the term used by the firm for their artificial rocks; latterly they used the term 'Pulhamite stone' for their terracotta.
3. A copy of this is held by the RHS Lindley Library, London.
4. A copy of this is held by the RHS Lindley Library. Lowewood Museum, Hoddesdon, have a photocopy of the same.
5. Information about the family is taken from S. Festing, 'Pulham has done his work well', *Garden History*, 12 (1984); 'Great credit upon the ingenuity and taste of Mr Pulham', *Garden History*, 16 (1988); A.J. Francis, *The cement industry 1796–1914*, 1st edn (Newton Abbott, 1978), pp. 91–109, 275–6; C. Hitching, 'James Pulham in Herts', Parts 1–5, *Hertfordshire Countryside* (Jan–May 2004) (*passim*).
6. J. Pulham, *The Builder* (5 April 1845), p. 160.
7. Hitching, 'James Pulham in Herts', p. 38.
8. J. Corfield, 'Pulham and Son', *Hertford and Ware Local History Society Journal*, 1 (1998), pp. 12–15.
9. Anon., Catalogue of the Great Exhibition, *Art-Journal* (1851), p. 303.
10. Anon., *Art-Journal* (1859), p. 28.
11. J. Davis, *Antique garden ornament*, 2nd edn (Woodbridge, 1998), p. 189.
12. Anon., *Art-Journal* (1851), p. 303.
13. Anon., *Art-Journal* (1862), p. 101.
14. Pulham, *Picturesque ferneries*, p. 74.
15. Anon., 'Garden Memoranda', *Gardeners' Chronicle* (1842), pp. 607–8.
16. Pulham, *Picturesque ferneries*, p. 72.

17. A. Lawrence, *The Aldenham House gardens* (Cambridge, 1988), p. 25
18. Anon., *Gardeners' Magazine* (2 February 1912), p. 106.
19. Anon., *Gardeners' Chronicle* (8 May 1920), p. 231–2.
20. Festing, 'The ingenuity and taste of Mr Pulham', pp. 101.
21. Pulham, *Picturesque ferneries*, p. 38.
22. John Phillips (1800–1874) wrote several books on geology including *Guide to geology*
     (1835), *Treatise on geology* (1837) and *Manual of geology* (1855).
23. Anon., *Gardeners' Chronicle* (28 January 1893), p. 101.
24. Pulham, *Picturesque ferneries,* p. 26.
25. Davis, *Antique garden ornament,* p. 191, quoting L. Jewitt, *Ceramic art of Great Britain*
     (1878).
26. Pulham, *Picturesque ferneries*, p. 47.
27. J.C. Loudon, *Encyclopaedia of Gardening* (London, 1825), p. 360.
28. Pulham, *Picturesque ferneries*, p. 8.
29. *Ibid.*, p. 29.
30. *Ibid.*, pp. 46–7.
31. E. Robinson, *The Garden* (journal of the RHS), 119 (1994), pp. 210–11.
32. Anon., *Gardeners' Magazine*, pp. 105–6.

Bibliography

Secondary sources
Anon., Catalogue of the Great Exhibition, *Art-Journal* (1851)
Anon., *Art-Journal* (1859)
Anon., *Art-Journal* (1862)
Anon., 'Garden Memoranda', *Gardeners' Chronicle* (1842)
Anon., *Gardeners' Chronicle* (1 January 1903)
Anon., *Gardeners' Chronicle* (8 May 1920)
Anon., *Gardeners' Magazine* (12 February 1912)
Corfield, J., 'Pulham and Son', *Hertford and Ware Local History Society Journal*, 1 (1998)
Davis, J., *Antique garden ornament*, 2nd edn (Woodbridge, 1998)
Festing, S., 'Pulham has done his work well', *Garden History*, 12 (1984)
Festing, S., 'Great credit upon the ingenuity and taste of Mr Pulham', *Garden History*, 16 (1988)
Francis, A.J., *The cement industry 1796–1914*, 1st edn (Newton Abbott, 1978)
Hitching, C., 'James Pulham in Herts', Parts 1–5, *Hertfordshire Countryside* (Jan–May 2004)
Jewitt, L., *Ceramic art of Great Britain* (London, 1878)
Lawrence, A., *The Aldenham House gardens* (Cambridge, 1988)
Loudon, J.C., *Encyclopaedia of Gardening* (London, 1825)
Pulham, J., *Picturesque ferneries and rock-garden scenery* (London, 1876/7)
Pulham, J., *Garden ornament, vases: terminals: pedestals* (illustrated catalogue, *c.*1925)
Pulham, J., *The Builder* (5 April 1845)
Robinson, E., *The Garden* (journal of the RHS) (1994)
Robinson, W., *Alpine flowers for English gardens* (London, 1870)
Robinson, W., *The English flower garden* (London, 1883)

Further reading
Elliott, B., ' "We must have the noble cliff": Pulhamite rockwork', *Country Life* (5 January 1982)
Garside, S., *Hoddesdon: a history* (Chichester, 2002)
Thomas, G.S., *The rock garden and its plants* (London, 1989)

CHAPTER NINE

A Victorian passion: the role of Sander's orchid nursery in St Albans

Harold Smith

Sander of St Albans
The Mighty Orchid King
Is filling all his boxes
For shipment in the Spring.
Punch

Introduction

In St Albans there is a road called Vanda Crescent (the name of a species of orchid) and another called Flora Grove, leading off from Camp Road (Figure 9.1). In nearby Dellfield a block of flats is named Laelia House (another species of orchid). On the opposite side of Camp Road there is a group of three mature purple beech trees and a couple of mature lime trees, and in the adjacent Cecil Road a block of old people's flats is named Orchid Court. These are virtually the only remaining traces of what was once claimed to be the largest orchid nursery in the world. The nursery was owned by Frederick Sander, born in Germany, granted the Royal Warrant as Royal Orchid Grower to Queen Victoria, and the man dubbed by *Punch* 'The Orchid King'.

There have been many fashions for plants: for auriculas in the sixteenth century, for tulips in the seventeenth century, for dahlias in the eighteenth and nineteenth centuries. But in Victorian times in Britain and Europe there was a fashion for orchids. It was brought about by a combination of factors: a fascination with the beauty and strangeness of the flowers and the way they grew; the age of imperial exploration, in which Europeans searched the world for plants and resources which would be of value to their countries; the popularity of science and the collecting, cataloguing and arranging of things from the natural world. It was made possible by advances in the construction of glass houses and

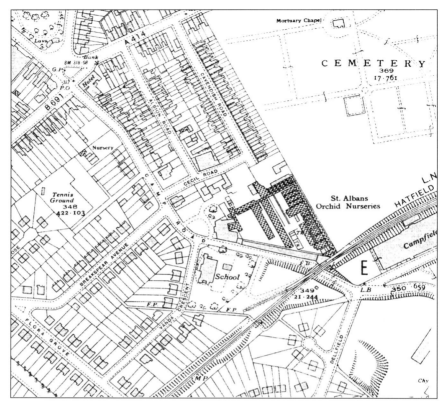

Figure 9.1 Detail of Ordnance Survey map sheet XXXIV.12, 25 inches to the mile, 1937, showing the reduced size of the nursery, and new housing in Vanda Crescent and Flora Grove

improvements in their heating; the use of Wardian cases to protect delicate plants in transit; the greater speed and reliability of steam ships transporting them; and later the publication by popular gardening magazines of information on their cultivation. And of course there were the wealthy patrons willing to pay almost any sum for the latest finds. A number of nurseries competed to supply the demand, sending out their own plant hunters and also buying from freelances, all of whom were in competition with each other. Sander's St Albans nursery was said to be the largest of them all.

The history of Sander's nursery can be seen to reflect the rise and fall of the Victorian fashion for orchids. Before looking at this fashion and the place of Sander's nursery in its story, it is useful to consider the history of orchids themselves.

Orchids

Orchids are one of the largest groups of flowering plants, distributed throughout the continents; those of horticultural significance grow mainly in the tropics, from sea level to mountain areas. Some are terrestrial, rooted in the soil; some are epiphytes, growing in trees and forming aerial roots to cling on to their supports and to absorb water and food; and a small group live on bare rocks. Generally their flowers are brightly coloured, often with pronounced shading or patterning, and the lower petal forms a pouch. A distinctive feature is that the sex organs are arranged on the same column, whereas in most flowering plants they are separate.

Orchids have a remarkably long documentary history: as long ago as 2800 BC the Chinese Emperor Shen Nung recorded their use in medicine. In the seventeenth century dried seed pods of the vanilla orchid were imported by the Spanish from Mexico to flavour hot chocolate and to use as a perfume.[1] The Dutch East India Company collected wild specimens, and explorers such as Drake, Bligh and Cook sent home plants. In 1731 the first tropical orchid was sent to England from the Bahamas and successfully flowered, but it was not until the end of the eighteenth century that the great European interest in orchids became established (Appendix 1).

One of the first descriptions of an orchid appeared in Curtis' *Botanical Magazine* in 1790, when an orchid from the Bahamas was flowered from material in the earth imported with other plants (Plate 9.1).[2] A similar story is told of William Cattley, who tried growing on a piece of packing material from plants sent to him and in 1818 flowered a magnificent plant which John Lindley of the Horticultural Society named *Cattleya labiata* in his honour. Kew listed fifteen exotic orchids in its collection in 1789, which had grown to eighty-four by the time the second edition of the *Hortus Kewensis* was published in 1813. In 1821 a third of the illustrations in Lindley's *Collection Britannica* were of orchids and five years later the Horticultural Society had a collection of 180 tropical orchids. In the early 1830s the sixth Duke of Devonshire was said to have caught 'orchid fever' on seeing an *Oncidium papilo*; he had Paxton design a conservatory for orchids (Figure 9.2), and sent John Gibson to hunt for them in Assam. By 1847 the Duke 'owned the finest collection in England'.[3] And it was in 1847 that Frederick Sander, who was to develop a similar passion for orchids, was born.

Figure 9.2 The great conservatory at Chatsworth. REPRODUCED FROM K. LEMMON, *THE GOLDEN AGE OF PLANT HUNTERS* (LONDON, 1968)

Figure 9.3 Sander and his wife in old age. REPRODUCED FROM A. SWINSON, *FREDERICK SANDER: THE ORCHID KING* (LONDON, 1970)

Frederick Sander

[Henry] Frederick Sander was born in Bremen. His father was a cask and barrel maker but his mother was related to the Kropp family, a branch of whom were nurserymen. At sixteen, Sander is recorded as leaving a nursery in Weimar, with an excellent reference, to work for Kropp at Erfurt (Appendix 2). From here he decided to go to England, arriving in 1865 or 1866 with the proverbial half-crown in his pocket. He worked for Ball's nursery in London and then for Carter's the seed merchants, where he met Benedict Roezl, a traveller, naturalist and plant hunter, and the man who introduced him to orchids and his life-long passion for them. He seems to have decided that orchids would be his life and that 'he must found his own company and begin importing them'.[4]

By the end of the 1860s he was an assistant nurseryman in St Mary Cray, Kent. The nursery bordered the estate of a wealthy partner in a paper mill and Sander apparently talked to his daughter, Elizabeth Fearnley, over the hedge. The humble nurseryman and the wealthy young lady (who was two years older than him) married in about 1870 or 1871. Sander must have been personable, determined, and promising as a businessman to have cut through the Victorian barriers of class, money and nationality and to have been accepted in this way; Elizabeth's father settled a large amount of money on her at her wedding.

The couple lived in Lewisham for the next few years, where Sander must already have been importing orchids and becoming an expert on them, as in 1875 he was corresponding on friendly terms with Professor Reichenbach, a world authority on orchids. In 1876 he bought up an established St Albans seed business (with the help of his wife's money) in George Street, in the oldest part of the city, and almost immediately began extending with seed-producing hothouses and a conservatory for fuchsias. He bought more land behind the shop for orchid houses and to raise seedlings but was obviously feeling constrained by the limited scope for expansion, for in 1882 he bought eight acres of land in Camp Road to found a new nursery (Figure 9.5). He also owned land on the north side of Hatfield Road, which later became part of Clarence Park. The George Street premises did not close until 1886, but by 1885 he had changed the style of his firm from 'seed merchant' to 'orchid grower'. Frederick Sander was in many ways the epitome of a Victorian self-made man, progressing from spade-hand to nursery owner in a foreign country in just a few years; he was by no means the only Victorian businessman to move up on the back of his wife's money!

The nurseries and the plant hunters

Although Sander's was not the first nursery in the orchid trade, it became the largest and the most important. At this time the cultivation of orchids and their propagation was not properly understood, so nurseries relied on importing large quantities of orchids, hopefully new and ever more exciting species and varieties, to supply their customers. They relied on plant *hunters* (used to distinguish them from plant *collectors*, the nurseries' customers) to find and send back the plants.

The first nursery to cultivate orchids on a commercial scale was Conrad Loddiges of Hackney, who traded for forty years and introduced many species, such as *Cattleya loddigesii*. Another famous London nursery was James Veitch and Sons, Royal Exotic Nurseries, one of whose plant hunters was Thomas Lobb, who was sent off to the Far East on a four-year trip in 1843. He explored the Malay Peninsula and Java, sending back many new orchids, such as *Phalaenopsis amabalis* and *Vanda tricolor*, and also many rhododendrons. He went out again at the end of 1848 and discovered further treasures; many of the plants of *Vanda coerula* he found died in transit but those that survived were sold for £300 each.

Close to the Veitch nursery in Chelsea was that of William Bull. A showman, he advertised his annual exhibitions in the daily papers, invited fashionable people to attend, and spread a brilliantly coloured awning from the nursery entrance so that patrons would not get wet if it rained, or scorched if it was hot. Hugh Low and Co. (with the advantage of a family member as a Rajah in Sarawak) and Messrs Charlesworth and Co. (who carried out extensive hybridising) were other nurseries whose names are commemorated in the names of the orchids they introduced. Another nursery specialising in orchids was the firm of B.S. Williams of Holloway, founded by a former gardener of a noted collector, Robert Warner.

Nurseries were in constant competition to introduce new species and varieties. When Low announced that his plant hunter had found *Dendrobium speciosissum*, which had been lost for forty-four years, Sander immediately stated that Claes Ericsson was sending home for him a consignment of the same plant. Sander was the first to flower the plant, beating Low by a fortnight, and receiving a Royal Horticultural Society Award of Merit for it. On another occasion, when bulbs of the new *Cattleya sanderiana* were about to be auctioned at Steven's, one of Sander's clients walked in with a plant in full flower; some complained at Sander's showmanship, but he gained over £2,000 from the auction.[5]

Competition between plant hunters, spurred on by their employers, was also intense. A story is told of William Arnold, employed by Sander, travelling out to Venezuela with a fellow passenger who said he was an engineer called White. Sander found out from 'intelligence' in the orchid world that White was one of Low's orchid hunters and sent a warning cable to Arnold in Caracas. Arnold confronted White with a drawn pistol in a locked cabin saying, 'Either you or me must not leave this cabin alive'; White surrendered.[6] Hunters would jealously guard the locations of their finds, deliberately mislead rivals, denude whole swathes of jungle of plants and destroy all traces of their presence. This ensured the rarity of the plants they found and maintained the high prices made at sales and auctions for the nurseries and for themselves. It led also to many orchids having to be 'rediscovered' years after their first introduction.

In 1909 the search was on for *Laelia gouldiana* (Plate 9.2), which had been discovered many years before by a Mr Theimer. To Sander's delight, he found that one of his orchid hunters, Louis Forget, had talked to Theimer before his death, learning that it came from a village called St Augustín in Mexico. This proved to be a common name! However, he eventually found the right village and then the orchid when, having accidentally stepped on the reflection 'of a bouquet of leaves and elegant branch of flowers' on the ground, he 'looked up and saw the first plant in full bloom'.[7] Sander introduced it in 1911 and the next year had over 7,000 flower spikes to cut for the Christmas flower trade: the cut-flower trade in orchids had by this time spread from America to Europe.

Sander at various times employed about forty plant hunters, more than any other nursery. Many were German, including William Arnold, Frank Klaboch, Kerbach, Mau and Carl Roebelin (although the latter may have been a German-speaking Swiss), who was to discover *Vanda sanderiana* in the Philippines, a plant which Reichenbach named in Sander's honour (Plate 9.4). The plants that Roebelin first saw were destroyed in the worst earthquake the Philippines had known but when Sander received a few dried specimen flowers he immediately cabled Roebelin to return and find more plants. This was especially urgent as he suspected Low had wind of them and was sending out his own hunters. Sander wanted not only the glory but also the financial reward for being the first to introduce it.

Sander employed Roezl, the man who introduced him to orchids, as a plant hunter in Central and South America where rare orchids he collected at 11,000 feet died as they were brought down to warmer levels. Later he went on to send up to eight tons of orchids a time back to England. Another was William Micholitz, who was sent to Burma and wrote back to Sander complaining eloquently of the hardships he and other plant hunters suffered: plague and cholera, poor food and accommodation, dust or humidity, and always enervating heat. They faced disease, tribal warfare, all sorts of natural disasters, bad communications, corrupt and cheating local officials and porters. Sander was as dictatorial with his plant hunters as he was with his other employees, sending letters and cables demanding more and more plants and that these be packed in a proper fashion. In one letter to Arnold he complained 'Found one *Masdevallia* alive in the whole crate … miserably packed … why put paper over the plants to take more air from them and nourish the cockroaches?'[8] It was not only the commercial loss that upset him but also the destruction of the orchids he loved.

The nurseries and their plant hunters operated in response to the demand by passionate collectors for fashionable orchids, but also drove this demand by their constant supply of new and exotic introductions. And of all the nurseries, Sander's was the one in the forefront of supply through the large number of plant hunters he employed and his own passion for new introductions. As previously noted, orchid cultivation was not well understood, and new plants were constantly needed. However, in the Victorian age there were many industrial and technological advances which made the transport and growing of tropical orchids easier.

Technological advances

The early explorers and plant hunters sent back their orchids and other plants by sailing vessels; the journeys were long and their arrival uncertain. As steam power replaced sail from the 1840s onwards the speed and reliability of sea travel improved but there were still losses; on one occasion Sander had cause to bemoan the loss of a ship with 177 cases of orchids. Early consignments of plants suffered from travelling through the tropics and then colder latitudes, and from the effects of salt air or lack of water. Nathaniel Ward's successful experiments with closed, glazed cases meant that from 1834 it was possible to transport many more plants in good condition, although it seems probable that the vast quantities of orchids imported were sent in packing cases in a semi-dormant state. But it still relied on the plant hunter being able to get the plants safely to port for shipping and being able to find the right packing materials.

Tropical orchids obviously needed warmth and humidity to prosper in the British climate. Heat in early greenhouses was supplied by stoves, which would often poison plants with their fumes. Steam heating was tried but was found to be difficult to control and eventually hot water heating was adopted. Hot water from a separate boiler house was circulated either in pipes running round the glasshouses or in trenches covered with gratings or, as in the orchid house at Copped Hall, Essex, in open troughs, to raise the humidity of the air. Glass was available only in small panes until the 1830s, when sheets of 'cylinder' glass up to thirty-six inches long became available, although the new glass had fewer impurities with no green tinge to protect the plants, so that summer shading became necessary.[9] The removal of tax on glass in 1845 meant that more and larger glass houses could be built, aided by the development of strong, light, wrought-iron glazing bars which were slimmer than wooden sections and so allowed in more light (Figure 9.4).

Wealthy orchid collectors became able to expand their collections and nurseries could keep the plants in better condition. Joseph Paxton, at Chatsworth in Derbyshire, experimented with different growing

Figure 9.4 A typically ornate Victorian conservatory. REPRODUCED FROM K. LEMMON, *THE GOLDEN AGE OF PLANT HUNTERS* (LONDON, 1968)

conditions and realised that many orchids came from higher altitudes and would grow better in more temperate houses. In time this would make it easier for the middle classes to aspire to their own collections. Later on, special pots (Maule's pots, which resembled modern strawberry pots) were made for amateurs to display orchids.[10]

Sander's new nursery elaborated on these technical advances. The *Gardeners' Chronicle* described the length of the new glass house (240–300 feet) as 'unheard of in the annals of orchid culture'. They admired the clever arrangement of heating pipes below the side ventilators of the coolhouses so they could remain open day and night and, by raising the centre of the side beds, help the circulation of warm air into the centre of the houses.[11] A similar layout had been adopted by Paxton at Chatsworth. In a later visit the magazine described the use of a large, sealed hot water tank in the middle bed of one house which helped to maintain an even temperature, and an arrangement of drilled pipes to spray water below the staging to maintain the required humidity.[12] By this time, twelve houses had been built with a total length of about 3,000 feet, ranging in width from 14 to 31 feet (Figure 9.5), and the

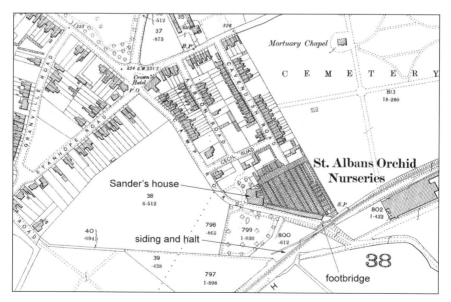

Figure 9.5 Detail of Ordnance Survey map sheet XXXIV.12, 25 inches to the mile, 1898, showing Sander's orchid nursery with its extensive glasshouses, and annotated to indicate his house, the railway siding and footbridge

nursery employed over 100 people. Many lived in the adjacent roads; numbers 45 and 47 Camp Road were named Cattleya Cottage and Laelia Cottage respectively.

Frederick Boyle, a traveller, naturalist and garden horticultural writer, visited in 1891 and later wrote up his impressions of the 'orchid farm' in typical Victorian flowery prose.[13] This was at the time that Swinson refers to as the 'high noon' of the St Albans nursery. There were about three acres of glass by this time, including show houses for tropical and cool orchids. Both were high, arched glass houses featuring tufa walls, studded with orchids, down which water ran into a pool at the base. A glazed corridor 400 feet long, hung with baskets of Mexican orchids, linked the show areas. The ends of some of the houses were being remodelled to make an entrance structure for visitors to step into directly from the train. A show pool for growing *Victoria amazonica* water lilies had been abandoned because of the numerous small black flies it produced (shades of Francis Bacon with his problems with 'frogs and flies' in the seventeenth century!). Boyle comments on the use of specially designed bricks in the paths, recessed to hold water to bolster the humidity while keeping one's boots dry. At this time, orchids were arriving in scores of cases a week.

Sander also made maximum use of Victorian transport technology for moving his orchids. His nursery in Camp Road was directly adjacent to the St Albans to Hatfield branch line which connected with the main rail line to Kings Cross. Visitors could arrive at the halt and walk across a footbridge straight into the nursery entrance. Sander had his own siding by the Camp Road halt (Figure 9.5), close to where Laelia House now stands, and his own orchid wagons, heated and ventilated, to bring in new orchids and to send plants to London for sale and distribution. Between 1895 and 1910 the railway timetable allowed for up to four stops a day at the siding, declining to one a day by 1919 and disappearing by 1922.[14] This could illustrate the decline in trade in orchids, and/or an increased reliance on motor transport. Coal for the nursery boilers was also delivered to the siding; orchids and coal were taken by horse and cart to the nursery entrance in Cecil Road.

A number of technological advances in Victorian times that helped in growing and transporting orchids were made use of by all the nurseries. Sander, by the scale of his operation at St Albans, provides a good reflection of the way in which these were used both to grow and display his orchids to the many customers who flocked to his nursery. Orchid collectors and enthusiasts also relied on these technological advances to grow and display their orchids.

The collectors

The Duke of Devonshire, with the vast resources of the Chatsworth estate behind him, has already been mentioned as one who was smitten by orchids and became an avid collector. Many others of the early collectors were wealthy men who had the resources to indulge in their passion. William Cattley was a merchant who collected other tropical plants as well as being one of the first enthusiasts to grow epiphytic orchids in his glasshouses in Barnet, between 1788 and 1835. He was also a patron of John Lindley, paying him a salary to describe and paint the plants in his collection. James Bateman built up a large collection in the early nineteenth century at Knypersley Hall, Staffordshire, keeping them there even when he married and built Biddulph Grange, with its magnificent gardens, a couple of miles away.[15] He employed George Skinner to hunt for plants for him, and published a book on Mexican and Guatemalan orchids in 1837. The Reverend John Clowes built up a collection at Broughton Hall, Manchester, which he left to the Kew collection when he died in 1846. Sir Charles Lemon of Carclew in Cornwall had a notable collection on which the young Lobb brothers, who both went on to become famous plant hunters, worked at an early age in the stove houses.

One noted collector, Mr Measures, having been prescribed rest by his doctor, bought a house in Streatham with seven acres and ended up with thirty-one orchid houses, under the control of the ex-orchid man from Chatsworth, and thirteen gardeners. At one auction of Sander's plants he bought a piece of *Cypripedium insigne* for 100 guineas (the first plant had been bought by Baron Schroder for 72 guineas), divided it over the years and refused an offer of 1,000 guineas for it. The most valuable orchid of them all was *Odontoglossum crispum* Frederick Sander, one plant of which was sold to Mr H.T. Pitt for £1,500 in 1904 (Plate 9.3). Pitt's rival for the plant was Baron Schroder, who out-bid him for another *Odontoglossum* at £1,250. The Baron grew and divided this over the years, keeping a specimen bulb and selling off divisions worth £3,000.[16]

Orchids were seen as a symbol of status in Victorian society. The Rt Hon. Joseph Chamberlain MP maintained thirteen glasshouses in his gardens in Highbury, Birmingham, most opening directly from his house, with one devoted solely to displaying orchids in bloom. When the House was sitting he had two buttonholes sent to London every day, preferably an *Odontoglossum*, which was his favourite.[17]

Chamberlain was one of Sander's clients but was deeply offended when Sander named a new introduction, *Cypripedium chamberlainianum*, after him. The orchid had long, dependent petals shaped like twisted screws; at the time, Chamberlain was unpopular for buying up small screw manufacturers in Birmingham and he took this as an insult. Sander's other clients read like a Victorian *Who's Who*. He claimed to be the only supplier to Nathaniel Rothschild at Waddesdon, travelling to Paris, Frankfurt and Vienna to sell to other branches of the family and apparently using their family motto *Concordia Integritus Industria*.[18] Other clients were Lord Salisbury and the Dukes of Devonshire and Marlborough; Sander often travelled to Blenheim on Sundays and the Duke sent him oak for the panelling of his new house at Camp Road as a sign of his esteem. He was awarded the Royal Warrant for supplying orchids to Queen Victoria and marked her Golden Jubilee with a vast bouquet of orchids seven feet high and five feet across which he personally delivered to Buckingham Palace, later watching the parade from the Rothschilds' house at Hyde Park Corner. He paid for the bouquet himself, for he loved England, he loved the beauty of orchids, and he loved the acclaim that this would bring to himself and his nursery. He even supplied orchids to the Pope.

The early collectors were wealthy men, many from the nobility, and most known to each other. They formed a network, meeting at shows, auctions and nurseries, seeing what was bought and, while trying to out-do the others, also exchanging information and plants. Sander's list of clients was an apt reflection of this, from royalty through the ranks of nobles and landed gentry to wealthy self-made men who had the time and money to spend on the latest fashions in plants.

The science and popularisation of orchids

The Victorian era was as much a period of science as of technology, with amateurs collecting fossils, minerals, and natural history subjects such as butterflies and birds' eggs. They sought to group and classify them: it was the age of Lyell, Huxley and Darwin, who predicted the existence of a moth necessary to fertilise a particular orchid from the shape of its flower.

'Official' hunters were dispatched by Kew and the Horticultural Society to find more orchids, to describe the conditions in which they grew, and bring back seeds as well as saleable plants. On occasions, plant hunters representing nurseries, private collectors and learned societies spied on and avoided each other in the same area.

John Lindley of the Horticultural Society was one of the first to classify orchids, listing 157 genera in the appendix to his *Collectanea Botanica*. By the time of his last work, the *Folia Orchidacea* in the 1850s, this number had grown to 1,343[19] and he estimated the total would be of the order of 6,000. The Horticultural Society (later the Royal Horticultural Society) set up an orchid committee and published a *List of awards to orchids*.

Sander played his part in the study and classification of orchids. He constantly sent material to Professor Reichenbach and to Kew for identification, extending their knowledge of species and varieties, but also gaining credit for his nursery and himself for introducing new plants to cultivation. He sponsored the *Reichenbachia*, a four-volume work on orchids published between 1888 and 1894 dedicated to Professor Reichenbach. The 192 plates were drawn and coloured with over twenty inks by the famous illustrator Henry Moon (who married Sander's daughter) and the whole project cost Sander over £7,000. The first volume was also dedicated to Queen Victoria and other volumes of the Imperial and Folio editions were additionally dedicated to other royal customers.

Fashions, in plants as elsewhere, spread downwards in society. More people became able to grow orchids as the cost of glasshouses fell, easier means of heating them became available, and more information on orchids' growing conditions was published. The major publications have been mentioned, but more accessible ones were published. Williams of Holloway brought out the *Orchid growers' manual* in 1852, with many later editions, and Veitch published the *Manual of orchidaceous plants* in 1887–94. The popular magazines of the day described new varieties, reported on the auctions of new plants and gave the ordinary gardener information on their cultivation; one volume of the *Gardeners' Chronicle* for 1883, as an example, indexed well over 100 articles on orchids. Even glasshouse manufacturers such as Messenger illustrated their catalogues with houses for cool or warm orchids. Sander again contributed to the popularisation of orchids with *Sander's orchid guide* and *Sander's list of orchid hybrids*.

Later events

The fashion for orchids declined in the early part of the twentieth century for a number of reasons. A fall in agricultural prices and land values at the end of the nineteenth century meant that landowners were less wealthy and had less money to spend on large, heated glasshouses. Labour was becoming more expensive and less easy to obtain as men could earn more in factories. A new generation of plant hunters like Kingdon Ward, Wilson, and Ludlow and Sheriff were introducing rhododendrons, shrubs and trees from cooler climates which could be grown outside and required less labour. Many notable gardeners now concentrated their interests on arboretums and American Gardens to display the plants coming in from the New World, and large shrubberies for rhododendrons and azaleas from Asia. And growing orchids had moved down the social scale.

Sander's nursery in St Albans was losing money, through his extravagance in constantly building and altering his premises, inefficient business methods and bad accounting; it is also suggested that his manager was dishonest. But the nursery that he had opened near Bruges in 1894 was flourishing, specialising in box topiary as well as orchids, and helped to keep the St Albans nursery going. The First World War

Figure 9.6 The remains of the packing and receiving buildings with Sander's house behind in 1968, before final demolition of the buildings. REPRODUCED FROM WHEELER AND STEVENS, *AROUND ST ALBANS* (2001), BY KIND PERMISSION OF TEMPUS PUBLISHING LTD

reversed matters, as St Albans had to send money by various routes to keep Bruges ticking over. When Sander died in 1919 his sons kept the St Albans nursery going but it declined without his drive and enthusiasm. The glasshouses were demolished in the 1950s and his house and the receiving and packing buildings eventually pulled down in 1968; a school was later built on the site (Figure 9.6). The specimen trees which had been planted in the garden of his house were saved by local people campaigning for Tree Preservation Orders to be issued.

Conclusion

The Victorian fashion for orchids was driven by a number of forces: the orchids themselves and the desire to own the latest and most beautiful or unusual; the nurseries and plant hunters who supplied them; the technological advances which brought them from overseas and which enabled them to be grown in the British climate; and the growth and spread of knowledge about them.

Frederick Sander embodied all of these factors in his nursery in St Albans. He employed more plant hunters and introduced a greater number of new plants than other nurseries. He made use of the latest available means to transport and grow these introductions; he contributed to the growth and spread of knowledge about orchids; he had the greatest range of famous and influential clients. All that he did was driven by his own passion for orchids: he loved them and wanted to grow them and show them off to all. Although so few traces remain of his extensive nurseries in St Albans, his most lasting memorial is that more than twenty species and varieties of orchids have 'Sander' as part of their name (Plate 9.4). The history of Frederick Sander and his orchid nursery in St Albans truly reflects the story of the Victorian fashion for orchids.

Notes

1. E. Hansen, *Orchid fever. A horticultural tale of love, lust and lunacy* (London, 2000), p. 62.
2. W. Curtis, *The Botanical Magazine; or flower garden displayed* … (London, 1790), pl. 116.
3. A. Swinson, *Frederick Sander: the orchid king* (London, 1970), p. 37.
4. *Ibid.*, p. 23.
5. *Ibid.*, p. 72.
6. *Ibid.*, p. 45; J. Davies, *The Victorian flower garden* (London, 1991), pp. 97–8.
7. Swinson, *Frederick Sander*, p. 192.
8. *Ibid.*, p. 54.
9. M. Woods and A.S. Warren, *Glass houses. A history of greenhouses, orangeries and conservatories* (London, 1988), p. 89.
10. Davies, *Victorian flower garden*, pp. 107–8.
11. Anon., 'New orchid houses', *Gardeners' Chronicle* (16 June 1883), p. 757.
12. Anon., 'Orchids at St Albans', *Gardeners' Chronicle* (15 March 1884), p. 342.
13. F. Boyle, *About orchids: a chat* (London, 1893), pp. 181–209.
14. R.D. Taylor and B. Anderson, *The Hatfield and St Albans branch of the Great Northern Railway* (Oxford, 1988), pp. 25–7.
15. P. Hayden, *Biddulph Grange, a Victorian garden rediscovered* (London, 1989), p. 10.
16. Swinson, *Frederick Sander*, pp. 176–7.
17. *Ibid.*, p. 108; Davies, *Victorian flower garden*, p. 101.
18. Swinson, *Frederick Sander*, p. 30.
19. W.T. Stearn (ed.), *John Lindley 1799–1865. Gardener, botanist and pioneer orchidist* (Woodbridge, 1999), p. 117.

Bibliography

Secondary sources

Anon., 'New orchid houses', *Gardeners' Chronicle* (16 June 1883)
Anon., 'Orchids at St Albans', *Gardeners' Chronicle* (15 March 1884)
Billings, T., *The Camp: a local St Albans history* (private publication, 2005)
Boyle, F., *About orchids: a chat* (London, 1893)
Curtis, C.H., *Orchids: their description and cultivation* (London, 1950)
Curtis, W., *The Botanical Magazine; or flower garden displayed…* (London, 1790)
Davies, J., *The Victorian flower garden* (London, 1991)
Fookes, M., *Made in St Albans* (private publication, 1997)
Hansen, E., *Orchid fever. A horticultural tale of love, lust and lunacy* (London, 2000)
Hayden, P., *Biddulph Grange, a Victorian garden rediscovered* (London, 1989)
Lemmon, K., *The golden age of plant hunters* (London, 1968)
Musgrave, T., Gardner, C. and Musgrave, W., *The plant hunters* (London, 1999)
Ritterhausen, W. and B., *The practical encyclopedia of orchids* (London, 2000)
Stearn, W.T. (ed.), *John Lindley 1799–1865. Gardener, botanist and pioneer orchidist* (Woodbridge, 1999)
Swinson, A., *Frederick Sander: the orchid king* (London, 1970)
Taylor, R.D. and Anderson, B., *The Hatfield and St Albans branch of the Great Northern Railway* (Oxford, 1988)
West, C., 'The orchid king of St Albans', *Hertfordshire Countryside*, 28 (August 1973)
Wheeler, A. and Stevens, T., *Around St Albans* (Stroud, 2001)
Whittle, T., *The plant hunters* (London, 1970)
Woods, M. and Warren, A.S., *Glass houses. A history of greenhouses, orangeries and conservatories* (London, 1988)

Appendix 1 – the chronology of orchids

2800 BC	Chinese Emperor Shen Nung refers to orchids in a book on medicinal use of plants
10th century	*The Orchid Book* by the Chinese scholar Kin-Sho lists orchid nurseries and areas where plants grow in the wild
16th century	Pods from the vanilla orchid sent from Mexico to Spain for flavouring chocolate
1731	*Bletia verecunda* sent from the Bahamas; it flowered the following year
1790	First description of an orchid in Curtis' *Botanical Magazine*
1798	Kew lists 15 tropical orchids in its collection
1818	William Cattley flowers *Cattleya labiata* from packing material
1825	14 out of 41 illustrations in Lindley's *Collectanea Botanica* are of orchids
1826	Horticultural Society has a collection of 180 tropical orchids
1834	Wardian case proved on round journey to Australia
1830s	The 6th Duke of Devonshire catches 'orchid fever'
1837	He sends Gibson to hunt for orchids. Paxton builds conservatory at Chatsworth. Around 300 species introduced to Great Britain by various orchid hunters
1840s	Nurseries such as Veitch, Low, Rollison importing in large quantities
1845	Glass tax repealed
1850	At a sale at Steven's auction rooms over 600 lots sold. Top price £9 for a plant
1851	Articles by Williams, 'Orchids for the millions', in *Gardeners' Chronicle*
1852	First successful hybrid by Dominey of Veitch's *Cattleya dominii*. Flowered in 1856
1852–8	Lindley's *Folia Orchidacea* published
1878	Two of the largest orchid consignments ever received – estimated at 2 million plants
1883	Index to *Gardeners' Chronicle* for Jan–June lists well over 100 references to orchids
1893	*Cattleya labiata* rediscovered by Forget
1898	Rediscovery of *Laelia jongheana*
1905	Rediscovery of *Cypripedium fairieanum*
1904	Sander sells *Odontoglossum crispum* Frederick Sander to H.T. Pitt for £1,500. Baron Schroder pays £1,250 for *Odontoglossum crispum Cooksonianum* and later sells divisions for £3,000

Appendix 2 – the chronology of Frederick Sander

1847	Born in Bremen
1863	Left a nursery in Weimar to go to Kropp's nursery in Erfurt for further training
1865 or '66	Arrived in England. Worked at various nurseries. Met Benedict Roezl
End 1860s	Assistant nurseryman in St Mary Cray. Met Elizabeth Fearnley
1870 or '71	Married Elizabeth Fearnley. Daughter born in 1871; first son born in 1874
1875	Importing orchids; corresponding with leading orchid expert Prof. Reichenbach
1876	Buys established seed business in George Street, St Albans. Extends premises, builds greenhouses for fuchsias and seed production
1877	As 'agricultural seed merchant', buys further land behind George Street
1879	Sends Arnold to South America and Carl Roebelin to the Philippines
1880	*Vanda sanderiana* (found by Roebelin) named in his honour
1881 or '82	Builds greenhouses for growing orchids and raising seedlings
1881	*Phalaenopsis sanderiana* discovered by Roebelin in the Philippines
1882	New premises in Camp Road, St Albans. George Street not closed until 1886. *Cattleya sanderiana* sold at auction for high price
1884	*Gardeners' Chronicle* article describes his nursery and 3,000 feet of glass houses
1885	Style of firm changed to 'Orchid grower'
1886	Title of 'Royal Orchid Grower' bestowed
1887–94	'High noon' of St Albans nursery
1887	Giant bouquet of orchids made for Queen Victoria's Golden Jubilee
1888	First volume of the *Reichenbachia* appears
1891	Frederick Boyle, traveller and journalist, visits and describes the St Albans nursery
1894	Opening of the Bruges nursery
1897	Awarded the Victoria Medal of Honour by the RHS
1903	Sander ill. St Albans nursery losing money and bolstered by Bruges
1904	Sells *Odontoglossum crispum* Frederick Sander to H.T. Pitt for £1,500
1911	Sander has serious operation
1914	Belgium invaded. St Albans has to support Bruges during the war
1919	Sander dies in Belgium following another operation
1922	War claims settled
1925	Sons divide up assets not required for running the business
1953	St Albans glasshouses demolished
1968	Remaining premises demolished

CHAPTER TEN

Clarence Park, St Albans – a late-Victorian public park

Harold Smith

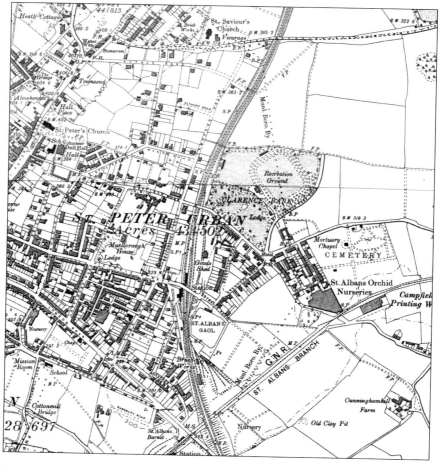

Figure 10.1 Detail of Ordnance Survey map sheets XXXIV.N.E. and S.E., 6 inches to the mile, 1899, showing Clarence Park on the east side of St Albans (not to original scale)

Introduction

Clarence Park is a small public park in St Albans, created in 1894 and given to the city by a wealthy local businessman at a time when St Albans itself was a small market town with some local industries such as straw-plaiting and brewing, but was also the home to a world-famous orchid nursery. The park (Figure 10.1) was made at the end of the Victorian period, which had seen a large number of public parks laid out in towns and cities around the country. In itself it is not remarkable, but it is an example which can serve to illustrate the history of Victorian public parks and some of the reasons for their creation. It is also a good example of that local Victorian philanthropy which contributed so much to the improvement of towns and cities.

Public parks in Great Britain

There had been a movement toward the provision of public parks through the nineteenth century. In 1833 the Select Committee on Public Walks had noted that, with increased building in towns, there was less opportunity for exercise and recreation in the open air. Later in the century the physical condition of those called on to fight in the Crimean and Boer Wars showed that the urban poor were suffering from a lack of good food, clean air, and body- and character-building exercise. There was thus a perceived need to provide public open spaces in addition to the commercial pleasure gardens, such as Vauxhall and Belle Vue, and the cemeteries and botanical gardens where the working classes could temporarily escape from their surroundings. However, early examples of public parks, such as the Derby Arboretum, designed by John Loudon in 1840, and Prince's Park in Liverpool, by Joseph Paxton (1842), were private developments, not provided by local authorities. One of the first municipal parks was Paxton's Birkenhead Park of 1843; both this and Prince's Park followed the example set by Regent's Park in London in using the green space so created to boost the value of houses developed nearby, thus neatly combining public good with private profit. The early parks charged admission fees but had free entry on half-days and Sunday afternoons to ensure the poor could have access.

Victorian social concerns

In addition to the Victorian concern about the physical state of the urban poor, there were also worries about their morals. Too much time and money was spent in public houses, partly for lack of anywhere else to go. This clearly had an adverse effect on family life, so dear to the hearts of the Victorian middle classes. The provision of museums, art galleries and public parks was seen as 'part of the desire to civilize the masses by making knowledge, culture and healthy exercise accessible' and was also 'aimed at undermining the effect of the public house'.[1] Derby Arboretum had been designed to educate visitors by guiding them through a display of labelled tree species which demonstrated the botanical orders. Crystal Palace Park, laid out in the 1850s, was also heavily influenced by a desire to educate the public, with its aquarium, model of a coal mine, and the series of models of prehistoric creatures. The early public parks tended towards the Gardenesque style, with sinuous paths winding between mounds and lakes. It was not until the 1860s that bright, formal bedding was introduced, following the example set by Paxton at Crystal Palace, so that 'the working classes could see a display of summer flowers without going to Kew'.[2] But the restrictions on opening times, admission charges, and prohibition of games in the early parks hardly encouraged the development of mind and body.

As well as worries about the physical, moral and educational shortcomings of the urban poor, there was always the shadow of civil unrest. The French Revolution was not so long ago, the Corn Laws had provoked riots and the Chartists were demanding an extension of the franchise. In the middle of the century the American Civil War upset trade, causing unemployment and subsequent civil disturbances, particularly in the cotton manufacturing areas of the north. Perhaps fresh air, some exercise of the right kind, and a little scientific education would make the mass of the people less inclined to be disenchanted with their lot.

Victorian philanthropy

There were many reasons, therefore, for attempts to be made to improve living conditions in towns and cities. Much of this was taken on by wealthy Victorian philanthropists, many of them non-conformists, whose social and religious beliefs inclined them towards practical ways of improving the living conditions of their workers. Edward Akroyd built Akroydon model village in West Yorkshire for his workers in the 1850s and Titus Salt built Saltaire factory and town, also in West Yorkshire, between the 1850s and 1870s.[3] By the end of the century, Lord Leverhulme had started the construction of Port Sunlight in Cheshire,

Bournville was laid out in the suburbs of Birmingham by George Cadbury, and New Earswick, North Yorkshire, built by Joseph Rowntree, followed in 1901. Their houses had private gardens with open spaces to give factory workers fresh air and open-air occupations. Philanthropy was also common in the horticultural world of the time. James Bateman built the church and parsonage at Biddulph, Staffordshire, designed by Edward Cooke, who also designed parts of his famous gardens, and nurseryman Harry Veitch paid for two church missionaries in Chelsea, founded the Gardeners' Orphan Fund, and worked assiduously on behalf of other gardeners' charities.[4]

The creation of public parks, and later in the century recreation grounds, was an important way in which the Victorians could improve the living conditions and the physical and moral status of the urban poor. At the same time society could be made safer for the middle classes, some entrepreneurs could make money from property development, and others could make their mark through their good deeds. How does Clarence Park, and its creator Sir Blundell Maple, fit into this picture?

Figure 10.2 Undated early postcard of Clarence Park, showing the drinking fountain, bandstand and lodge. REPRODUCED FROM J. CORBETT, *PICTURE POSTCARDS OF OLD ST ALBANS* (1996), BY KIND PERMISSION OF THE PUBLISHERS, MMA

The establishment of Clarence Park

Clarence Park was given to the city of St Albans by Sir Blundell Maple and opened in 1894. There were public open spaces in the city before then, but no public park, and none specifically intended for recreation. The reason for the gift was that the St Albans Cricket Club wanted a permanent ground. They played their matches on Bernard's Heath, on the northern edge of the city, and felt that they had no security of tenure or facilities such as a pavilion. With no possibility of affording their own ground, they approached Sir Blundell, a successful businessman who had a large estate at Childwickbury, just north of St Albans, and he agreed to provide a ground for them.[5] The initial scheme expanded into a

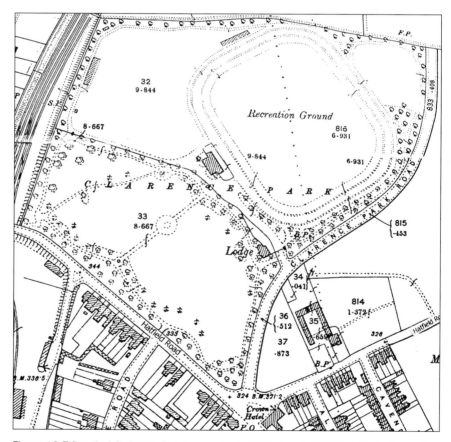

Figure 10.3 Detail of Ordnance Survey map sheets XXXIV.8 and XXXIV.12, 25 inches to the mile, 1897, showing Clarence Park and recreation ground (not to original scale)

combination of sports facilities of about sixteen acres and a public park of nine acres (Figure 10.3).

Part of the land, with its southern boundary on Hatfield Road, was purchased by Maple from Earl Spencer, who had large landholdings in the district, and part from Frederick Sander, the orchid nurseryman, whose nursery was on Camp Road, on the other side of Hatfield Road. As part of his agreement to the sale of the land, Spencer stipulated that a road be built along the eastern border of the park for housing development, now called Clarence Road. The park was to be given to the people of St Albans, and the local council was to be responsible for its upkeep.

Sir Blundell Maple the businessman

Who was Sir Blundell Maple and why did the cricket club go to him for help? He was the son of John Maple, who founded the famous London furniture store (Sir Blundell's full name was John Blundell Maple but he did not use his first name). John Maple had set up shop in Tottenham Court Road in 1841, by then one of the centres for furniture manufacturing and the sale of household goods in London. He became wealthy, sending his son to school and then on to King's College, London. When Blundell Maple graduated in 1861 he went straight into the family firm, at the bottom, and 'studied detail, from an envelope to a ledger. I grounded myself in prices ...'.[6] He was made a partner in 1870, became an equal partner in 1879, and seems to have been the driving force in the firm's expansion. Over the years it expanded greatly; eventually Maples occupied twenty acres from Tottenham Court Road across to Gower Street, fronting the Euston Road and served by the new Metropolitan Railway. They imported woods, textiles and other materials, manufactured on site most of the furniture and household goods that they sold, and furnished royal palaces, country houses, upper- and middle-class houses. Blundell Maple was a typically wealthy, successful Victorian businessman who knew every detail of his business, worked hard, and provided employment for over 2,000 people.

Maples believed in quality goods and craftsmanship, training up apprentices in all trades and providing hostels for their workmen: a Maple training in the retail world was akin to a Kew training in the horticultural world. Blundell Maple was proud of this aspect of his achievements, but this did not prevent him, in 1888, being called before the 'Sweating Committee', a House of Lords enquiry into sweated labour and excessive profits made by retailers on the backs of small firms of craftsmen. He refuted any suggestion that his firm did not pay fair wages, that staff were bullied or worked excessive hours, that he bought cheap and sold dear under his own name: he pointed out that the average length of service for staff was over ten years. He was cleared by the enquiry: it was apparent that he was a strict but fair Victorian master, who did as much as or more than contemporary business standards required him to do for his workers (Figure 10.4).

Sir Blundell Maple the public man

Feeling he could do more for working people as a politician, Blundell Maple first got elected to the London County Council and then, in 1887, succeeded, in his second attempt, at becoming an MP for Dulwich. He was probably the first shopkeeper to sit in Parliament but the papers of the day were supportive of the well-known retailer and horse breeder. He called for Parliament to pass legislation to help the working classes to find work, opposed a Bill to tax horse vans (Maples had its own large fleet) and attacked a Bill to introduce compulsory early closing. He later exposed the scandal of excessive profits made by middlemen purchasing horses for the British Army abroad.

Figure 10.4 Blundell Maple at the time of the 'Sweating' enquiry. REPRODUCED FROM H. BARTY-KING, *MAPLES FINE FURNISHERS: A HOUSEHOLD NAME* (1992), BY KIND PERMISSION OF QUILLER PUBLISHING LTD

He was knighted in 1892. It was seen as a fitting tribute to a Victorian businessman who worked hard, upheld high standards in his work and life, and was fair and benevolent to his workers by the standards of the time. He expected no more of any man than he would do himself (Figure 10.5).

Sir Blundell Maple the philanthropist

Blundell Maple became a wealthy man as the firm expanded. He bought Clarence House, in Clarence Terrace on the Outer Circle of Regent's Park, as a town house near to his firm. He also purchased the large estate of Childwickbury, near St Albans, where he built up a stud farm into the largest horse-breeding establishment in Britain. For serious racing purposes he bought Falmouth House at Newmarket. He was a familiar figure in St Albans, driving his own coach from Childwickbury to the railway station for the train to London (and probably in a shorter time than in today's traffic).

But he also put some of his money into philanthropic schemes. In 1883 he chartered special trains to take 1,800 St Pancras schoolchildren on a summer excursion to Childwickbury Manor, where they were entertained with 'steam merry go rounds, swings and coconut shies, and

Figure 10.5 Sir Blundell, knighted in 1892. REPRODUCED FROM H. BARTY-KING, *MAPLES FINE FURNISHERS: A HOUSEHOLD NAME* (1992), BY KIND PERMISSION OF QUILLER PUBLISHING LTD

a sumptuous Tea'.[7] He did the same the following summer for Marylebone children. He paid for a Christmas dinner for 270 poor people of St Albans, held in the Assembly Room and followed by a musical entertainment provided by the Clarence Minstrels, a group of Maples employees.

In 1889 he set up the Clarence Athletics Club, with grounds in Mill Hill, north London, for his employees, where they could meet away from the firm to enjoy sports and the annual Sports Day. In 1897 he established, on land that he owned in Harpenden near Childwickbury, an almshouse of sixteen one-bedroom flats and a convalescent home for eight males and eight females, for old or incapacitated former employees.

When the University of London established a Dispensary, later to become University College Hospital, close to his store, he helped to raise money for it. His rich friends donated £900, and £700 a year came from the collecting boxes of the 'Maple or People's Fund' he had placed in local cafes and pubs. For his local people of St Albans, he paid in 1893 for the building and equipping of the Two Sisters Hospital for Infectious Diseases, as a memorial to his two younger daughters who had died in infancy.

It is clear why the cricket club members approached him for help. He was a well-known, popular, rich and successful businessman who was known for his philanthropy, love of sport, and assistance to his local community. It is clear, too, that the St Albans Council were also appreciative of his intention to give land and money for not only a sports ground but also a public park and recreation ground, something the city lacked. This is not really surprising as St Albans was not a large industrial city, the countryside was near to hand, and there were already areas of public land where people could meet, play games, and even hold pageants. St Albans, then still a small country town, had obviously not felt the social pressures that larger industrial towns and cities had. But a public park would help raise the status of the town and its council.

Clarence Park: its form and use

The local benefactor would obviously have had strong views on how the land that he had paid for was to be used. As the initial suggestion for the development came from the local cricket club, the main part of the recreation ground would be a cricket field. In a letter to the City Council in 1892, setting out his proposals, Sir Blundell wrote, 'As regards the cricket ground, I consider cricket and athletics sports as great factors in

demanded was soon occupied by substantial detached and semi-detached Victorian and Edwardian villas, many with front balconies overlooking the park: one has recently been on the market at over £1.25m, reputedly the one-time home of Samuel Ryder, the seedsman and golf fanatic. Similar houses were built along the north side of the park (Figure 10.7). St Albans soon began to spread east along Hatfield Road with the arrival of printing firms from London to the area known as Fleetville, and other factories and housing followed. The development of Clarence Park and its adjacent housing was clearly one factor in the expansion of St Albans, at least for the more prosperous middle classes, as the development of Fleetville further east along Hatfield Road was based around factories and working-class housing.

A contrast with a twentieth-century park

But it was not only in Victorian times that parks were created to provide public open space, to act as examples of philanthropy, and to add to civic status. In 1932 Verulamium Park was created on the south-west corner of St Albans. A study of its creation can help to show whether the

Figure 10.7 Detail of county photomap sheet 695 showing Clarence Park, 1973, annotated to indicate features in and around the park. © HERTFORDSHIRE COUNTY COUNCIL, 2006

Victorian park movement was unique or merely part of a pattern of provision of public facilities.

The creation of Verulamium Park

World War I showed that Britain's youth were still suffering from the same lack of exercise and open-air activities that had been noted in Victorian times. In 1927 the St Albans Council received a letter from the Hertfordshire Playing Fields Association on the need to supply playing fields, saying that funds were available from the National Playing Fields Association and the Carnegie Trust. By April 1929 the Council, considering the preservation of open spaces in or immediately adjacent to the city, had negotiated with the Earl of Verulam to sell them the freehold of St Germain's Farm, extending to 103 acres, for £6,500. This would also include part of the site of the Roman town of Verulamium, which would be preserved from any possible development (Figure 10.8). The Council were trying to borrow the money from the Ministry of Health on the grounds that this was to be permanent open space –pleasure and recreation grounds, including playing fields.[13]

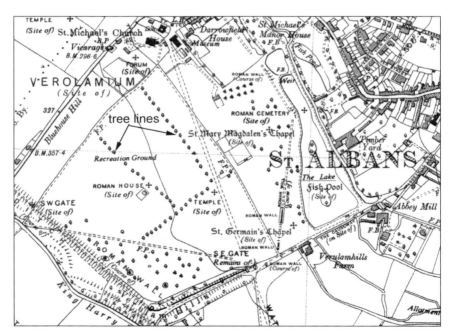

Figure 10.8 Detail of Ordnance Survey map sheet XXXIV.SE, 6 inches to the mile, 1951, showing Verulamium Park with the lake and tree lines of earlier hedges (annotated)

This was a time of great unemployment and the Council determined to carry out public works to help alleviate it. In 1921 some of the unemployed had been given work on widening Waverley Road in the city and 'from that time until the 1930s similar council relief schemes continued to be needed'.[14] In July 1930 a report was presented on the provision of a grant from the Unemployment Grants Committee (UGC) towards the construction of a boating lake, paddling pool, etc., on water meadows near to the river Ver in the new park. Conditions imposed by the UGC stipulated that men must be recruited through Labour Exchanges, 75 per cent must be ex-service men and materials must be British where possible. Some of the men who were employed were said to be Jarrow marchers.

By September 1931 the lake and paddling pool scheme was two-thirds complete and, although the economic situation was bad, it was decided that the scheme was to be carried through in its entirety, otherwise many would be thrown out of work and the project would eventually cost more. In March 1932 it was decided that boating for hire could not go ahead on the lake as the conditions of the grant from the UGC said that activities must be non-revenue generating. As with Clarence Park, there were no formal beds, but also no major shrub or tree planting; instead many of the existing trees and hedges were kept and still indicate the boundaries of the old fields (see Figure 10.8).

While this work was going on, Sir Mortimer and Tessa Wheeler were engaged in extensive excavations of Verulamium; a temporary, and later a permanent, museum was built to display their finds. When the excavations were finished, a tea-room was built. It was also agreed that public toilets should be built, as the nearest ones were in the Town Hall, over half a mile away – uphill! A number of football and hockey pitches were laid out, with tennis courts and cricket squares for the summer; by 1934 changing rooms were to be built.

Verulamium Park did not have the same effect on the development of the city as Clarence Park. But it did bring more people to that part of the city and helped to link St Michael's village more closely to the city centre. Fishpool Street, running parallel to the north-east side of the park, of where it was said no girl would admit to her boyfriend that she lived, began to lose its bad reputation and has since been 'gentrified'. The building of Bluehouse Hill past the western edge of the park also contributed to the later expansion of St Albans, while at the same time marking a definite boundary between town and country. The park's construction undoubtedly provided work for many men at a time of great need and provided the growing city with public open space which protected the architectural treasures of Verulamium from the possible threat of future development. It still provides a magnificent setting for the Abbey and has contributed to the enjoyment of the citizens of St Albans and to the status of the city as a centre for tourism and pilgrimage.

In the second half of the twentieth century both parks fell victim to cuts in public expenditure as, across the country, public parks became seen as public liabilities rather than symbols of civic pride. Staffing and maintenance were reduced and outsourced to try and reduce the load on local financing. However, both parks have benefited in more recent years from more money being spent on them. In Clarence Park, with the help of the Heritage Lottery Fund, the fountain was restored and the bandstand replaced, although no longer thatched or so 'curly'; the pavilion has also been refurbished. Both parks now have children's play areas with brightly coloured play equipment, as children are now encouraged to enjoy themselves in public places! (Plate 10.2) Clarence Park has recently been awarded Green Flag recognition as a clean, safe and well-appointed play area.

Conclusion

Clarence Park has been shown to be a good example of a late-Victorian park. It was given to the city by a successful and wealthy local businessman who stood for the Victorian values of hard work for a fair day's wage, and who believed in helping those less fortunate than himself. It was given as a philanthropic gesture to meet the needs of the local community. In it were many of the features of a typical park of the time – the bandstand, exotic trees, areas for walking and decorous amusement – along with the recreation ground for physical exercise and social and moral improvement through team games of cricket, hockey and football. There were few formal flowerbeds, but that would not have been unusual by this time as much of the fashion for bright carpet bedding was past, and upkeep was becoming a major concern. It had a pronounced effect on the development of the city through the development of housing along its borders. It also soon proved to be a charge on the rates, which would not have been uncommon, in spite of the councillors' optimism when it was first mooted.

training fruit trees. The two end piers were rusticated with a simple pointed brick top, similar to some gateposts at Packwood House, Birmingham.[17] There is no evidence of any work to the end piers, leading to the conclusion that there were no walls extending from them on the east and west sides. Below the pointed brick coping, in the indent between the supporting piers, was a course of bricks set in the 'dog-tooth' pattern, below which was a course of corbelling (Plate 11.1).

At its highest point the wall was only eight and a half feet (nine feet with the coping). This was relatively low for a north wall that traditionally had the greenhouses built on the sunny south side and the 'back sheds' on the shady north side. The wall would have restricted not only the height of the greenhouses and the sheds but also the height to which the fruit trees trained on it could be grown.

The main entrance to the fruit garden was through wrought-iron gates in a brick arch set in a cypress hedge 300 feet long (Figure 11.7). Leading from the arch were nearly 140 cordon pear trees, planted in two rows and trained into a tunnel over iron supports which stretched for 60 yards, almost the entire length of the garden, towards the greenhouses (Plate 11.2). The hedges on the west and east sides were Western red cedar.

Figure 11.6 The rose garden, c.1927. FROM THE QUEENSWOOD SCHOOL ARCHIVES

Wormald built an impressive range of eight greenhouses, four of them from the Skinner Board Company of Bristol. The company had a patent for a 'wire tension' system, enabling curved roofs to be made with flat glass held together with bronze clips. This meant that there were no glazing bars, thus allowing more light into the greenhouses.

In the sales particulars of 1923 the greenhouses are listed as 'a Carnation house, Palm house, two Peach houses, Vinery, Melon and Tomato houses, Cyclamen house and ranges of Heated and Cold Frames'. On the wall next to the greenhouses were fan-trained peaches and nectarines.

The vegetable garden and orchard

Heavy wooden gates in the arch in the north wall opened into the vegetable garden, an area of approximately two acres extending round the north and west sides of the fruit garden (Figure 11.8). It was enclosed on the west side by iron railings, with kissing-gates at either end, which extended from the south-west corner of the fruit garden to the staff cottages near Sheephouse Hill. Inside the railings were planted damson and plum trees.

On the outside of the north wall were the 'back sheds', containing

Figure 11.7 The south entrance to the fruit garden, c.1925. FROM THE QUEENSWOOD SCHOOL ARCHIVES

the potting shed, boiler house (below ground), trap shed, pony stable, tool and barrow sheds and store rooms.[18] Planted against the wall beside the back sheds were four Morello cherry trees trained in fan shapes, and below them frames for growing violets.

Between the fruit and vegetable gardens and the drive an acre of land was planted as an orchard. The lodge at the northern end was converted into a gardener's bothy, with a mess room and another bedroom built alongside.

The staff

Records show that by 1917 Wormald was employing Mr Richard Lay, an experienced domestic gardener aged forty-one, as his Head Gardener.[19] Wormald's granddaughter wrote in her memoirs that 'most of the male gardeners were called up, and we had to have either rather tough or old women'. Wormald was not the only person who had to employ women; Kew Gardens employed thirty women gardeners to replace the conscripted men.[20]

Recruitment for the army started immediately after war was declared on 4 August 1914. Initially it was for men between the ages of nineteen and thirty years, but within three weeks this had been extended to the

Figure 11.8 The arch in the north wall, *c.*1915–20. REPRODUCED BY KIND PERMISSION OF JOANNA MARTIN

age of thirty-five years. By mid September 500,000 men had volunteered to fight and by the end of the following year that number had increased to two million.

In his book *The English Garden* Charles Quest-Ritson writes that 'the immediate effect of the First World War on gardens and gardening was undramatic'.[21] But surely this cannot be the case, as there is evidence that the effect was felt from the largest garden to the smallest allotment almost immediately. At Chatsworth, Derbyshire, they were left with twenty men and the garden deteriorated fast;[22] at Heligan, Cornwall, the usual twenty-two outside staff were reduced to eight, and the emphasis was on food production.[23]

The effect can also be seen quite clearly in the pages of the *Gardeners' Chronicle*. In early August 1914 there were four or five columns of 'Situations Wanted', with men looking for work in gardens, and by November the same year this had been reduced to approximately two columns. At the same time the employers in 'Situations Vacant' looking for garden staff increased from only one column in early August to five columns in September.

The school leaving age was thirteen years at the time so there was the potential to employ young boys in the garden, but training them would have been a thankless task, since there was every possibility that they would enlist to fight when they reached the age of eighteen years.

Because of the shortage of labour the Board of Agriculture and Fisheries set up a scheme in January 1917 called 'Employment of German Prisoner Ploughmen', which employed prisoners of war to work in agriculture. Hertfordshire was one of the first counties to set up the scheme[24] and Edward Wormald employed several prisoners in his fields, probably from the camp at Hatfield.[25]

The effects of the War on the development of the garden

Sheepwell was a typical 'small country house' and estate built just at the start of the First World War and, as such, the war probably had a far greater effect on the creation of the garden than is first apparent. Edward Wormald was a man who liked to have the latest innovations and followed popular trends. The sales particulars of 1923 inform us that his house had every modern convenience: central heating, electric lift, telephone, gas supply, electricity generator and garages; and also the newly fashionable additions to a house: a loggia and a garden room.

The most popular style of house in the early twentieth century was the mock-Tudor or Tudorbethan. The style featured regularly every year at the Ideal Home Exhibition between 1910 and 1939, the half-timbered detached house winning the Ideal Home competition for design in 1912.[26] This was exactly the type of house built by Wormald.

His love of innovation can be seen in his choice of a modern type of greenhouse from the Skinner Board Company and by his possession of a wireless, a feature which only started to appear in people's homes in the early 1920s, but which was recorded in his granddaughter's memoirs of her time at Sheepwell between 1915 and 1924. Even his choice of flowers indicated his desire to have the latest plant introductions. One of Wormald's descendants has a photograph of his grandchildren standing in front of a large dahlia border at Sheepwell. Dahlias had become 'show' flowers but they regained their popularity as garden flowers just prior to the war, when there was a trend towards spiky or ball-headed plants in borders, partly as a result of the dahlia 'trials' run by Reginald Cory at Dyffryn, South Wales.[27] In addition, the orange roses in Wormald's rose garden were a relatively recent addition to the rose colour palette.[28]

Although there does not seem to have been a problem in building the house, the garden did not contain the hard landscaping that one would associate with a house of this size, bearing in mind the amount of money spent on the house and Wormald's love of gardening. It might be expected that features such as paths, pergolas, garden buildings, terraces and walls would have been built in brick, to echo the building materials of the house, but apparently no such work was ever carried out.

Perhaps the formality of certain garden styles of the period did not suit a mock-Tudor house set on the edge of natural woodland. The rustic summerhouse and arbours did not look out of place, and there was a trend towards gardens with an open prospect and natural gardening.[29] William Robinson believed that a beautiful or well-placed house should not be cut off by a terrace wall;[30] Jekyll and Weaver that 'where Nature has been lavish with her wild charms the signs of the hand of man should be suppressed'.[31]

Wormald had several of the garden features mentioned in the book *Gardens for Small Country Houses* by Jekyll and Weaver, which had been published in 1912. These included the lily pond, the urn, the fruit pergola and climbing plants on the house.

What garden features there are do not seem to reach the same high standard used when building the house. The lily pond, a popular early

nineteenth-century garden feature, would normally have been
surrounded by high-quality paving; instead it was surrounded by a
moulded brick edging and grass; Jekyll and Weaver devoted a whole
chapter to lily ponds and stone paving in their book. The ha-ha, with its
wood and wire-netting barrier, was not as visually effective as it would
have been with a brick retaining wall. The back sheds were wooden, not
brick as one would expect; surely a fire hazard near the boiler house?

The only feature in the garden affording a glimpse of what Wormald
may have intended in his garden was the wall of the fruit garden, which
would have been built by a skilled bricklayer. Although this one brick
wall did not reach the recommended height for the north wall of a
kitchen garden, the whole length of the outside and the two end piers,
which would have been seen only from the vegetable garden, were
decorative, and most of that was hidden behind the back sheds.

What of the other three boundaries of the fruit garden, the south,
east and west sides? Jekyll and Weaver recommended beech and
hornbeam as excellent for kitchen garden hedges,[32] but Thomas Mawson,
another garden designer, advised that the kitchen garden should be
enclosed by walls or good high hedges. However, he warned that
hedges, which needed constant trimming, were not as effective as brick
walls which, while being more expensive to build, were more economical
in the long run because fruit could be trained on them.[33]

In a typical walled garden the acid-loving fruits, the Morello cherry
and redcurrants, would have been grown on the north-facing sides of the
north and south walls. At Sheepwell, because there is no south wall, fruit
could only be grown along 112 feet of the north-facing side of the
(north) wall, the remainder of that being taken up by the back sheds. A
south wall of the same length would have afforded an additional 300
feet. There was no east-facing wall for the sweet cherries, early plums,
apples and figs, and no west-facing wall for the peaches, greengages and
early pears.[34]

There are other instances of kitchen gardens being bounded by
hedges rather than entirely walled. For example, at the Palace House,
Beaulieu, Hampshire, the kitchen garden has two brick walls and two
hedges, but these were designed to ensure that the views from the house
and the lake would not be spoiled by brick walls. Not only was this not
necessary at Sheepwell, as the fruit garden was sited well away from the
house and screened by the rose garden, but there were also very good

reasons why the scope to grow fruit and vegetables should be maximised. There was pressure by the Government on the public to provide home-grown food, as blockades at sea prevented the importation of food, on which the public had become dependent. Although it had probably always been intended that produce from Sheepwell should be enjoyed not only at Sheepwell but also at their home in Berkeley Square, this became a necessity when war broke out. As well as the family, there were at least ten live-in staff at Berkeley Square,[35] in addition to the gardeners and their families, the housekeeper, and numerous guests at Sheepwell. Fresh fruit and vegetables would have been packed in baskets to be taken by pony and trap to Potters Bar station and then by train to London.

So why did Wormald, who could clearly afford the best, substantially restrict his ability to grow fruit and vegetables at Sheepwell by planting hedges instead of building walls? One reason might be that, as the estate was only going to be used for two months of the year, it did not warrant the expense of landscaping such a large garden. However, it does seem strange that, with so much money having been invested in the house, the same standard was not applied to the garden, although a considerable amount of money must have been spent on roses and the greenhouses.

A more compelling explanation would be that the supply of raw materials had dwindled, and they were becoming difficult to obtain; factories had gone over to producing items for the war and, as a consequence, all unnecessary building work was severely restricted. Was it as a result of his not being able to get bricks that he decided to plant fast-growing hedges to protect his new garden?

With the scarcity of building materials it must have been a considerable advantage to Wormald, when he was creating his garden and estate, that there were already five cottages, a lodge and a farmhouse on the land. It is difficult to imagine, in view of the restrictions, how he would have provided the necessary accommodation for his labourers and gardeners without these buildings.

Although we may never know whether Wormald had entertained greater ambitions for his garden which were not realised, the fact remains that, in spite of the difficulties presented by the First World War, Wormald created a delightful garden. However, after the war the way of life which he and many other country house owners had enjoyed became more and more difficult to sustain. He and his family continued to enjoy the house and garden until 1924, when it was sold to Queenswood School of Clapham, South London, who were looking for larger premises outside London. The school continues to enjoy the gardens created by Wormald in the early twentieth century and since 1992 they have been open to the public under the National Garden Scheme one weekend in May when the rhododendrons are in bloom.

Acknowledgements
I would like to thank the following people: Dr Wendy Bird, Queenswood School Archivist, for enthusiastically supporting my research; Maurice Hoare, retired Queenswood Estate Manager, whose personal knowledge of many original features of the garden was invaluable; Dr Joanna Martin, descendant of Edward Wormald, for allowing me access to the memoirs of Lady Sheelah Treherne and family photograph albums; and Mr T. Bygrave, builder, for sharing his knowledge of brickwork.

Notes
1. HALS, PC/267 a and b, Enclosure schedule and map, North Mymms, 1778/1782.
2. P. Kingsford, 'A history of Gobions in the parish of North Mymms, Hertfordshire', in P. Kingsford, R. Bisgrove and L. Jonas, *Gobions Estate North Mymms, Hertfordshire* (Brookmans Park, 1993), p. 10.
3. Private collection, memoirs of Lady Sheelah Treherne: unpublished property of Oona Methuen-Campbell.
4. Private collection, Treherne, 'Memoirs'. Three of Wormald's grandchildren, including Sheelah, the author of the memoirs, lived permanently with their grandparents after both their parents died within a week of each other in August 1917. Sheelah later became Lady Sheelah Treherne.
5. *Ibid.*
6. HALS, DE/X269/B37, sales particulars Leggatts estate, 1906.
7. T. Musgrave, C. Gardener and W. Musgrave, *The plant hunters*, 2nd edn (London, 1998).
8. W. Robinson, *The English flower garden*, 14th edn (London, 1883), p. vii.
9. G. Jekyll and L. Weaver, *Gardens for Small Country Houses*, 6th edn (London, 1912), p. xvii.
10. Jekyll and Weaver, *Gardens*, p. 147.
11. A. Page, *In Queenswood gardens* (published privately Queenswood School, 1924/5), p. 15.
12. RHS Lindley Library, *Gardeners' Chronicle*, 1915.
13. Knight, Frank and Rutley archives, London, sales particulars Sheepwell House, 1923.
14. B. Elliott, *Victorian gardens* (London, 1986), p. 21.
15. Page, *Queenswood gardens*, p. 17.
16. *Ibid.*, p. 17.
17. Jekyll and Weaver, *Gardens*, p. 201.
18. Knight, Frank and Rutley archives, sale particulars.
19. HALS, Kelly's Directory 1917, p. 114.
20. R. Desmond, *Kew* (London, 1995), p. 309.
21. C. Quest-Ritson, *The English Garden: a social history* (London, 2001), p. 228.
22. Duchess of Devonshire, *The garden at Chatsworth* (New York, 2000), p. 94.
23. T. Smit, *The lost gardens of Heligan* (London, 1998), p. 174.
24. P. Dewey, *British agriculture in the First World War* (Oxford, 1989), p. 120.
25. HALS, Wartime Agricultural Executive Committee report, 1917.